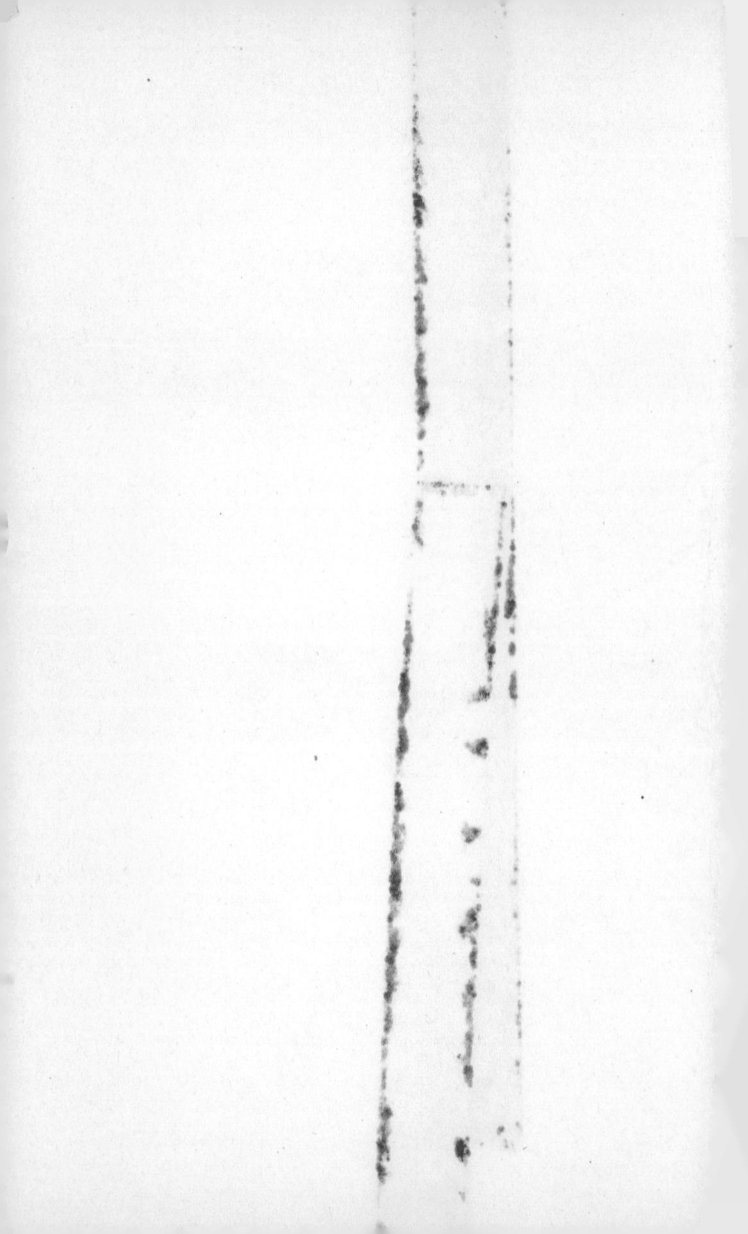

THE HOME UNIVERSITY LIBRARY OF MODERN KNOWLEDGE

250

THE DEVELOPMENT OF ENGLISH LOCAL GOVERNMENT 1689–1835

CONTENTS

Oxford University Press, Amen House, London E.C.4

GLASGOW NEW YORK TORONTO MELBOURNE WELLINGTON
BOMBAY CALCUTTA MADRAS KARACHI LAHORE DACCA
CAPE TOWN SALISBURY NAIROBI IBADAN ACCRA
KUALA LUMPUR HONG KONG

Printed in Great Britain

The Development of English Local Government

1689–1835

SIDNEY AND BEATRICE WEBB

With an Introduction by

SIR GEORGE CLARK, D.LITT., F.B.A.

Being Chapters V and VI of
'English Local Government:
Statutory Authorities for Special Purposes'

LONDON
OXFORD UNIVERSITY PRESS
NEW YORK TORONTO
1963

INTRODUCTION

SIDNEY and Beatrice Webb were eminent historians but they did not come to the study of history by the customary road. Neither of them was ever a full-time student at a university or went through a formal course of historical lectures and examinations. They began their famous partnership as social reformers. Beatrice developed her method of social study in the eighteen-eighties by working for her cousin Charles Booth on his great co-operative survey of London. Sidney was trained in the government service and studied law. When they set out jointly on their work for social reorganization they both believed in the effectiveness of ordered knowledge, or social science based on full information, and so they were investigators first and made their plans when their investigations seemed sufficiently complete. But they found that no survey of the existing state of society could explain the evils that they meant to remedy; it was necessary to discover how those evils had arisen. So the Webbs became historians not from any interest in the past for its own sake, but because they were intensely interested in the future.

What they embarked upon was not mere historical study but exploration. In most of the subjects that concerned them the available historical literature was pitiably inadequate. The main themes of British historical studies had been connected with the central organs of the state, the Crown and parliament, their constitutional development on the one hand, the policies which they had pursued on the other. For some periods, especially for the Middle Ages, a fuller picture of society as a whole was aimed at, but not for the eighteenth century, the period which the Webbs most urgently wished to understand, because it was that century which seemed to have strewn the country with much of the debris that they meant to clear away. They studied not merely 'the state', but the tangle of half-forgotten institutions among which people lived their ordinary lives, the parish and the county, the manor and the borough, their officers and their procedure, or rather they studied a prodigious number of parishes and counties, of manors and boroughs, of officers and procedures. They imposed order on this endless variety. Even with their astonishing industry the two of them could not have carried out this research, in libraries and in muniment rooms and laywer's offices all over the country, alone. They applied the method of survey and employed a team of assistants, not very large but well chosen and admirably directed. The result was their history of local government in England from the Revolution of 1688 to the Municipal Corporations Act of 1835, nine volumes published between 1906 and 1930.

This series of volumes was equally remarkable for its severely scholarly method, for its wealth of entertaining details and for its bold sweep of interpretation. Nor did it stand alone. The Webbs themselves buttressed it with other books, of which the most notable was their history of trade unionism. Other historians, in closer or more distant alliance with them, followed the same lines. From its early days their London School of Economics was a busy historical workshop, with a character of its own running across diversities of opinion. It had its own links with the continent, for instant through Élie Halévy. In the first quarter of the present century it seemed as if the method of survey might soon be fruitfully applied to still wider fields, such as the history of professions, of private associations, of education and of the family in its many aspects.

Very likely the promise of those years will yet be fulfilled; but for the present attention has been diverted to more specialized methods and to other fields. Economic historians, responding very rightly to the demands of economic thought, have concentrated on such matters as investment, the history of prices, the fluctuations of trade, and the movements of population. The two great wars have brought political history back into something like its old primacy. Ironically enough it is in the study of the eighteenth century, the Webb's chosen field, that historians are most clearly aware of a change in their point of view, but they date back the beginning of the change no further than 1929. This is the change associated with the name of Sir Lewis Namier. He and his numerous followers made parliament the centre of their studies, with individual biography as their instrument. In this they harked back from the sociological point of view, but in their exhaustive study of records they carried on a good deal from the earlier practice of the method of survey. Their debt to the Webbs may indeed turn out on examination to be considerable. The Webbs, in their systematic way, distinguished between the structure of local government and its functions. Even if it is a mere coincidence that Namier's first academic home when he settled in England was the London School of Economics, he may still have derived something of his conception of the structure of politics from it indirectly, and also something of his insight into the eighteenth-century political scene. The indirect influence of the Webbs' work at home and abroad cannot easily be estimated, but it has not been small.

That their direct example has not been more extensively followed is not due to any disappointment with the harvest of sociological history. Other historians did indeed detect some faults in the *History of English Local Government*. Sir John Clapham, who belonged to the individualist liberal tradition, was disposed to be more indulgent than the Webbs to the errors of the past, and he made some cogent criticisms of the view of the Industrial Revolution which underlay much of what they wrote about local government. He found traces of the over-idealized and already superseded belief that in England before the Industrial Revolution 'the great bulk of the inhabitants were independent producers owning the instruments and the products of their labour'. He showed that at least in some passages the Webbs assigned this Revolution to a date too early to fit in with any acceptable opinion as to what precisely it was. He corrected some of their statements about birth-rates, death-rates and population. The sum of these and similar criticisms, however, does not convey that the book as a whole is misleading or unsound, or indeed more imperfect than a pioneer work on this scale is bound to be. After making his points in a review of one of the volumes Clapham concluded quite simply by calling it 'this great book'.[1]

If any fault of the Webbs did interfere with the reception of the book, it was nothing worse than a failure of showmanship. One after another the volumes appeared in dismal dark blue bindings with a puritanical sobriety of lay-out. The seventh and most original of them, the one which Clapham reviewed, had a title, a cheerless title, as Tawney wrote, which was enough in itself to repel the reader: *Statutory Authorities for Special Purposes*.[2] Indeed it seemed as if the authors were transferring to literature the system with which legend credited them in politics, where their proceedings were so unobtrusive as to be almost subterranean. The Preface to that seventh volume begins with the sentence: 'To most people, if not to all, the chief interest of this book will lie in the last two chapters, which analyse the development of English Local Government from the Revolution to the Municipal Corporations Act.' Thus modestly did they announce a first-rate piece of research and writing, and thus, by stowing it away at the end of a volume of 500 pages, did they make sure that for more than a generation no one but exceptionally resolute students should read it.

It is not too late to give these chapters the chance of which their authors inadvertently cheated them. They are reprinted in the pages which follow here. Since they were written to form a unity in themselves,

[1] *English Historical Review*, xxxix (1924) 285 ff.

[2] Though it was the seventh to be published its place in the series is fourth.

scarcely any changes have been needed in presenting them as a separate book. The first two sentences have been re-arranged, but without any addition or subtraction. In two or three other places small adjustments have been made in the text. Some of the footnotes have been shortened by the deletion of illustrative or supplementary matter not strictly needed to support the argument. That is all. The two chapters, as the Webbs wrote them, will not be mistaken for anything less than masterly.

G. N. C.

PUBLISHER'S NOTE

THIS work originally appeared as Chapters V and VI of Vol. IV of *English Local Government* by Sidney and Beatrice Webb, the volume being entitled *Statutory Authorities for Special Purposes* (Longmans, Green, 1922). For permission to reproduce the material in its present form we are grateful to Frank Cass and Company Ltd. and to the Passfield Trust. Messrs. Frank Cass now publish *English Local Government* by Sidney and Beatrice Webb in eleven volumes, with additional essays by B. Keith-Lucas, G. J. Ponsonby, L. Radzinowicz and W. A. Robson (1963). The original nine volumes—*The Parish and the County*, *The Manor and the Borough* (2 vols.), *Statutory Authorities for Special Purposes*, *The Story of the King's Highway*, *English Prisons under Local Government*, *English Poor Law History*, *Part I*, *The Old Poor Law*, and *Part II*, *The Last Hundred Years* (2 vols.)—have been expanded by the addition of Vol. X, *English Poor Law Policy*, and Vol. XI, *The History of Liquor Licensing in England*, previously published separately.

PUBLISHER'S NOTE

This work originally appeared as Chapters V and VI of Vol. IV of *English Local Government* by Sidney and Beatrice Webb, the volume being entitled *Statutory Authorities for Special Purposes* (Longmans, Green, 1922). For permission to reproduce the material in its present form we are grateful to Frank Cass and Company Ltd, and to the Passfield Trust. Messrs. Frank Cass have recently reprinted *English Local Government* by Sidney and Beatrice Webb in eleven volumes, with additional material by B. Keith-Lucas, G. J. Ponsonby, [illegible] and W. A. Robson (1963). The original nine volumes—*The Parish and the County*; *The Manor and the Borough* (2 vols.); *Statutory Authorities for Special Purposes*; *The Story of the King's Highway*; *English Prisons under Local Government*; *English Poor Law History Part I: The Old Poor Law*, and *Part II: The Last Hundred Years* (2 vols.)—have been expanded by the addition of Vol. X: *English Poor Law Policy* and Vol. XI: *The History of Liquor Licensing in England* previously published separately.

Chapter One

A CENTURY AND A HALF OF ENGLISH LOCAL GOVERNMENT: THE OLD PRINCIPLES

WE have completed our survey of English Local Government from the Revolution to the Municipal Corporations Act—so far, at least, as constitutional structure is concerned. We now proceed to summarize in two chapters the outstanding characteristics of this period, whether manifested in the decay of the old or in the evolution of new principles of government.

We may first explain the significance of these particular years. When we turned to the subject of Local Government, nearly a quarter of a century ago, our object was to describe the organization and working of the existing local governing authorities, with a view to discovering how they could be improved. We realized from the outset that a merely statical investigation of what was going on around us would reveal little or nothing of the lasting conditions of disease and health in the social organizations that we were considering. We knew that, in order to find the causes of their imperfections and the directions in which they could be improved, we had to study, not only their present but also their past; not merely what they were doing but also how they had come to be doing it. Somewhat naïvely, we accepted as our starting-point the beginning of the nineteenth century. But after a year's work on the records, it became apparent to us that the local institutions of the first quarter of that century were either in the last stages of decay or in the earliest years of infancy. We saw that it was impossible to appreciate the drastic innovations of 1834–6, and their subsequent developments, without going much further back. After some reconnoitring of the seventeenth century, we decided that the Revolution of 1689 ranked, in the evolution of English Local Government, as the beginning of a distinct era which continued until the Reform Bill of 1832.

The best way of presenting to the reader the extensive and multifarious changes described in our volumes, will be first to discover and analyse the main principles—the ideas that governed men's minds, the traditional concepts still potent in constitutional organization—inherited in 1689 from previous centuries and embodied in the local institutions of the eighteenth century. We shall therefore describe in this chapter (i) the 'Obligation to Serve,' and to serve gratuitously in the discharge of local public duties; (ii) Vocational Organization as the very basis of government; (iii) the principle of Self-Election or Co-option; (iv) the Freehold Tenure of profitable office; (v) the conception of property, and at the outset landed property, as an indispensable qualification for, if not actually a title to, the exercise of authority; and, as explaining the absence of anything that could be called a system of Local Government, and the utter lack of uniformity or consistency, (vi) the predominance of local customs and the Common Law as the very basis of the whole. In the next chapter we shall set forth the gradual evolution of a new set of principles arising out of the circumstances and thought of the new age: principles destined to become dominant in the Local Government of the nineteenth century.

A Policy of Non-intervention by the Central Government

At the outset of our analysis appears, not any ancient principle, but a new policy, arising with dramatic suddenness out of the Revolution of 1689. A summary end to 'arbitrary interference' with 'local liberties' was one of the most important results of the dismissal of the Stuart dynasty. For more than a hundred years from that date, King and Parliament adopted a policy of indifference as to what the various local governing authorities did or abstained from doing. The interference of the Privy Council, and even that of the Courts of Law and the Assize Judges, sank to a minimum. In contrast alike with the centralized administration that was being built up, especially as regards poor relief, between 1590 and 1640, and with the arbitrary 'regulating' of Municipal Corporations of 1683–8, the King's Ministers after 1689, it is scarcely too much to say, deliberately abstained from any consideration of the Local Authorities; and hardly ever found themselves driven to come to any decision on the subject of their activities or their powers. The Justices of the Peace, between the Revolution and the Municipal Corporations Act, enjoyed, in their regulations, an almost complete and unshackled autonomy. Unlike a modern County Council making by-laws, Quarter Sessions was under no obligation to submit its orders for confirmation to the Home Secretary or to any other authority. Moreover, the Justices were, in their own Counties, not only law-makers, but, either collectively or individually, themselves also the tribunal to adjudicate on any breaches of their own regulations. Again, the Juries of the Manor, of the Court of Sewers, of the Hundred and of the County, were always 'interpreting' the local customs, and restricting or extending the conception of public nuisances, active or passive, according to contemporary needs, or new forms of the behaviour of individual citizens and corporate bodies; whilst the inhabitants in Vestry assembled, or the little oligarchy of Parish Officers, were incurring (and meeting out of the ancient Church Rate) expenditure on all sorts of services according to local decision, without any one having any practical power of disallowance. As for the Municipal Corporations, they regarded their corporate property, their markets, their tolls, their fines and fees, as well as their exemptions and privileges, as outside any jurisdiction other than their own. When, in the course of the eighteenth century, it became necessary or convenient to invoke Parliamentary authority for the enforcement of new regulations, or the levying of new imposts, this usually took the form, not of a statute of general application, but (as we have described in the present volume) of literally thousands of separate Local Acts. These peculiar and little studied emanations of national law were not devised by the Government or by its central departments, but were spontaneously initiated and contrived by little groups of the principal inhabitants of particular areas; they were debated and amended in the House of Commons, not by committees of impartial persons, but mainly by the representatives of the Boroughs and Counties concerned; and as we have described in the Introduction to this volume, it was not until the very end of the eighteenth century that the 'Lords' Chairman' began to insist on inserting clauses safeguarding what he considered to be the interests of the public at large. Thus, the special epoch dealt with in our description of the Parish and the County, the Manor and the Borough and the Statutory Authorities for Special Purposes, is a definitely bounded period, extending over more than a century and a quarter, of something very like an anarchy of local autonomy.

No System of Local Government

During the eighteenth century the anarchy of local autonomy was heightened by the fact that there was nothing that could be regarded, either in theory or practice, as a system of Local Government. There was, as we have described in the foregoing volumes, a confused network of local customs and the Common Law, of canon law and royal decrees or charters, interspersed with occasional and unsystematized Parliamentary statutes. Out of this confused and largely unexplored network, there had emerged four distinct organs of government: the Parish, the County, the Manor and the Municipal Corporation—not to mention the anomalous Commission of Sewers—to which was added, in the course of the eighteenth century, a new type described in the present volume—the Statutory Authority for Special Purposes. These distinct organs of government are found superimposed one on the top of the other, at different periods of history, for different purposes, by different instruments and with different sanctions. Alike in origins and in areas, in structures and in powers, they are inextricably entangled one with the other. What is common to them all is that not one of them was, or claimed to be, a system of Local Government. If any of the Dutch gentlemen who landed at Torbay with William the Third had asked a Lord Lieutenant, a High Sheriff or a Justice of the Peace to describe 'the Local Government of England', he would have met with a blank ignorance of any such order of things. The Rulers of the County would have thought of themselves not as Local Authorities at all, but as the deputies of the King, with an obligation to provide what was requisite for the King's soldiers, to hold the King's Courts, to maintain the King's peace; having a general commission to govern their own County as they thought right, and especially to supervise all other citizens in fulfilling their respective obligations. The peers and country gentlemen who consented to spend some of their leisure, in and out of Parliament, in performing these tasks, would have been aware that the City of London was wholly exempt from their control; and that up and down the land there existed many Cities, Boroughs, Franchises and Liberties which successfully claimed to exclude this or that particular Court or official jurisdiction. But these were mere exceptions to the normal government exercised by the landed gentry of the Kingdom. The suggestion that there existed any kind of lawful autonomy in the fifteen thousand

Parishes and Townships would have seemed to the country gentleman, at the end of the seventeenth century, an absurd and a dangerous contention. The two or three hundred Municipal Corporations would have accepted their status of exceptional privilege with complacency. They would have cited in proof their diverse Courts exercising jurisdiction over this or that area, entirely independent of the County; their infinitely varied constitutions, derived indifferently from charters, statues or immemorial custom, and frequently amended by their own by-laws, without intervention on the part of Parliament or the Government. The Lord of the Manor, on the other hand, would have told the curious inquirer that, as a landowner, he had, by immemorial usage, Courts of his own; that in these Courts his tenants were compelled to appear; and that he himself, or his steward, was always anxious to agree with them on any matters of common concern. He might have added that there were such things as Juries of his tenants, with certain rights to give verdicts, to declare the local customs and even to present him before his own steward for failing to conform to these customs, or for permitting the continuance on his property of any public nuisance. The Parish Constable, Overseer or Surveyor of Highways, far from feeling himself a member of a Local Authority, would have complained that he was compelled to serve without payment in an unpopular office, exacting from him much time and labour, at the beck and call of any interfering Justice of the Peace. Finally, the Churchwarden would have been puzzled to know whether he belonged to a secular or to an ecclesiastical hierarchy; and how far he was compelled to obey, on the one hand the archdeacon and 'the Ordinary', or on the other, the little group of 'principal inhabitants' in Vestry assembled. But not one of these personages would have regarded himself as forming part of anything that could be called a system of Local Government. He could hardly have conceived even of the existence of any such system. The very term, Local Government, was not in use before the middle of the nineteenth century.[1] Throughout the seventeenth and eighteenth centuries and right into the nineteenth century, the greatest county personage or the humblest parishioner stood on his personal status, whether that status was, in the main, one of authority over other men, as in the case of the County Justices, the Municipal Magistrates or the Lords of Manors; or, in the main, one of graduated subservience to superiors within an hierarchy, secular or ecclesiastical, as in the case of the Parish Constables, Overseers, Churchwardens, the citizens called out on the service of Watch and Ward in the town streets or the labourers summoned to Statute Duty on the country roads.

The Obligation to Serve

It was, indeed, this principle of obligation to render public service, a principle coming down from time immemorial, that was, and remained far into the

[1] We find the phrase 'local self-government' becoming current in the second quarter of the nineteenth century, largely through its use by Von Gneist and J. Toulmin Smith. From this, in the third quarter of the century, seems to have sprung the phrase 'local government'. It is difficult to

eighteenth century, the axle round which revolved all old-established local institutions, whether manorial or parochial, of the Borough or of the County. The particular obligations might rest on local custom or on the Common Law; they might be embodied in grant or charter, in general statute or, in later times, in a Local Act; they might attach to individuals or corporations, or be appurtenant to the ownership of particular estates. But however these obligations arose, they included, not merely a duty to obey, but also a direct charge on the will to act. They involved not only personal responsibility to a superior, but also such power over other persons as was incidental to the due performance of the public service. Thus, however men might differ in faculties and desires, or in status and fortune, they were all under obligation to serve in one way or another. It was, for instance, taken for granted that every respectable male resident was under legal obligation to undertake, without salary or other remuneration, one or other of the customary or statutory offices of Manor, Parish or County.[1] Though the method of selection varied, both by statute and at Common Law, we find a widespread local custom that each office ought to be served in rotation by all parishioners, qualified according to certain traditional requirements. 'In some places,' said Chief Justice Holt in 1698, 'people are to be Constables by house-row,' or rotation among occupiers. 'As it is an office of

believe that this cannot be found, here and there, at an earlier date; but it was certainly not until the middle of the nineteenth century that it came into common use. We notice it in a leading article of the *Times* on 15 December 1856.

[1] *The Parish and the County*, By S. and B. Webb, p. 16.

great burden,' wrote Thomas Gilbert in 1786-7, of the office of Overseer, 'it generally goes by house-row in rotation through the parish.' 'In fact,' summed up Dr. Burn in 1764, 'the office goes by rotation from one householder to another'—in 'indiscriminate rotation,' records another observer, 'among all those whose occupations render them liable to the office'. It was, in fact, at the end of the seventeenth century, still no part of the conception of local administration that there should be anything of the nature of what we should now call official staffs; that is to say, the voluntary and whole-time employment of persons at salaries and wages, to perform specified functions. Every service requisite for the simple life of the Manor or the Parish fell, in ancient times, within the duty imposed, as an incident of tenure or status, upon one or other inhabitant, either permanently or for a brief term in rotation with his neighbours. Nor was this universal obligation to render public service limited to individual residents or property owners. It was inherent in the very right to exist of corporate bodies of every kind. To the medieval statesman we may imagine that the Municipal Corporation, like the Manor itself, was primarily an organ of obligation, by means of which, in particular localities, the services required by the King might most conveniently be performed and could most easily be exacted. Similarly, in the eye of the law, neither Parish nor County was an organization for local self-government. On one plane the Parish, on another the County, was essentially a unit of obligation. It was the Parish, in some cases in succession to the Manor, and not any of its officers, that was liable for the upkeep of the church fabric, as well as of the churchyard; for compliance with this and that statutory obligation; and for the maintenance of its own part of the King's Highway. The officers and Courts of the County were, on their own plane, merely devices by which the obligations of the County itself were performed, and through which they could be enforced, whether these obligations related to the furnishing of the *posse comitatus* to put down any resistance to the maintenance of the King's Peace, or in later times to the militia raised for national defence; to the upkeep of the County Bridges without which there could be no free passage for the King and his men; to the keeping of the common gaol which was the King's, or the accommodation of the King's Judges when they came to hold the Assizes. Far from constituting any system of local self-government, the Courts and Sessions of the County Justices, and the services of the County officials were, from the standpoint of constitutional law, only instruments within the County for the proper keeping of the King's Peace, for the due execution of the King's writs, for the enforcement of the decisions of the King's Judges, for the exact and punctual payment of the various revenues due to the King, for the keeping of the King's prisons and the King's Courts, and for the maintenance of the great bridges without which the King's Highway could afford no convenient passage through the Kingdom.

It is this principle of personal obligation, on which the whole of English Local Government was based, that affords the explanation of the great bulk of the administration being, even so late as the eighteenth century, cast in what today seems the strange form of presentment and indictment, traverse and trial, sentence and fine or estreat. In the Manor and the County we find innumerable varieties of presentment which particular officers, or particular Juries of various kinds, from Sewers and Leets to Franchises and Hundreds, and finally the Grand Inquest for the County as a whole, were always being charged to make. It was by means of these presentments, and the cumbrous legal proceedings which they initiated, that all derelictions were dealt with, whether the ordinary breaches of the law by private individuals, the short-comings of parochial and manorial officers, the failure of Parishes to maintain their highways, their pounds and their stocks; the neglect of Franchises and Hundreds to keep the peace, whereby damage had been done; and equally the derelictions of duty of the County itself in failing to keep in repair the County Gaol or the County Bridges. What today emerges in the agendas and minutes of boards and councils as reports of committees and resolutions appeared, two or three centuries ago, as the proceedings of courts of justice, in the form of presentments, indictments, traverses, forfeitures and sentences.[1] It is, indeed, not

[1] The local bodies, says Maitland, were not 'the representatives of unorganized collections of men: they are the representatives, we might almost say, of corporations. . . . The same word (*comitatus*) serves to describe both the County, the geographical district, and the assembly. . . . The King's itinerant Justices from time to time visit the Counties; the whole County (*totus comitatus*), i.e. the body of freeholders stands before them; it declares what the County has been doing since the last visitation; the County can give judgment; the County can give testimony; the County can be punished

too much to say that, at the close of the seventeenth century, in the Courts of the Manor or in the Court of Sewers, the inhabitants of every surviving Manor, and of nearly every area liable to be flooded, including all the landowners and frequently the Lord of the Manor himself; and, at the Quarter Sessions and Assizes, all the Parishes and Hundreds, and at the Assizes all the Franchises, Liberties and Municipal Corporations, and even the County itself, represented by their unpaid and compulsorily serving officers, were, one or other of them, always in the dock, as defendants in nominally criminal proceedings, on which they were perpetually being amerced or fined. This, indeed, was the customary and regular procedure of the Local Government of the period.

The same notion of obligation elucidates what was understood by the conception of nuisance, which swelled into so large a part of the framework of law in which the ordinary citizen found himself. A nuisance implied a breach of obligation. If every person fulfilled his lawful duty, according to the customs of the Manor and the Common Law, no one would do or suffer anything to be done to the annoyance of his neighbours. Any breach of this fundamental obligation was therefore a nuisance, active or passive. Thus, the redress of nuisances came to include the remedying of every conceivable neglect or offence, from eavesdropping and disorderly drunkenness to the use of false weights and measures or the sale of unwholesome food;

by fines and amercements when the County has done wrong; if the County has given false judgment, the County can be summoned to Westminster' (*The Constitutional History of England*, by F. W. Maitland, 1919, p. 43).

from filth and stench, and neglect to pave, up to riot, sedition and recusancy. 'Cows, horses, sheep, pigs, dogs,' we are told, 'all required regulation, and had it.' Pigs, as the most perverse of animals, required the firmest and most rigorous handling; and hundreds of folio pages of Jury orders and presentments relate to swine alone, and their numerous misdeeds and nuisances, their 'eating corn in the market', and their nameless desecrations of the churchyard. But the worst of all nuisances, because it cut at the root of common order, was the refusal to serve in any of the customary offices, a breach of obligation which was accordingly visited with exemplary fines.

The Inequality in the Incidence of the Obligation to Serve

The democratic conception of the equality of all men in the service of the community was, it is needless to say, entirely absent from the general obligation to undertake public office still embodied in the old-established local institutions of the eighteenth century. This was partly due to the intimate association of the obligation to serve with the traditionally vocational basis of English society, political as well as industrial —a point we shall presently elaborate. But apart from this intimate association of public duties with particular vocations, the various obligations fell only lightly on men of property, and much more heavily on the humbler ranks of society. The peer, by reason of his dignity; the Member of Parliament, or the Justice of the Peace, on account of his office; the practising attorneys and barristers; the ministers of religion (originally of the one and only Church, and later also those of recognized nonconformist denominations), as well as the members of the three powerful corporations of physicians, of surgeons and of apothecaries, enjoyed a common, although not exactly uniform, exemption from service in such onerous and unpleasant offices as Parish Constable, Overseer of the Poor, or Surveyor of Highways.[1] And although it may have been theoretically doubtful whether any duly qualified person could lawfully refuse to be made a peer, to be elected to the House of Commons, or to be included in the Commission of the Peace, there was practically no obligation of attendance in Parliament, whilst an unwilling Justice might always refrain from 'taking out his dedimus', without which he could not act. It is an interesting sidelight that the only County office which was at once compulsory and expensive, that of the High Sheriff, was always imposed, unless occasionally a County personage deigned to accept it, on one of the minor gentry. Moreover, any well-to-do citizen, even if he could not claim exemption by status, might always buy exemption, either through the purchase of a 'Tyburn Ticket', or by merely paying a fine.[2] Finally, however onerous and unprofitable may have been the office of Constable, Overseer, Churchwarden or surveyor, it was accompanied by a little brief authority over fellow-citizens, a satisfaction denied to the still humbler inhabitants who had to carry out the

[1] For the detailed qualifications of this summary statement see *The Justice of the Peace*, by Richard Burn (first edition, 1754), under the headings of the several officers.

[2] *The Parish and the County*, pp. 19, 63.

orders of the Parish Officers in the town streets or on the country roads.

The Continually Increasing Inadequacy of the Principle of Obligation to Serve

Among the many reasons for the rapid acceleration of the decay of the Manor and the Municipal Corporation, for the distorted growth of Parish and County government, for the chaotic multiplication of Statutory Authorities for Special Purposes, and for the corruption and inefficiency characteristic of all these local institutions during the eighteenth and early nineteenth centuries, we know of no cause more universal and significant than the increasing inadequacy of the principle of obligation to serve as a method of local administration. We do not suggest that this principle of individual responsibility, and this obligation of personal service for the common good, is in itself objectionable. To many idealists it seems not only an attractive but also an ennobling social doctrine. As we shall indicate later on, it was a moral disaster that the public duties and obligations of citizens, as distinguished from their private interests and needs, should have been, by the Utilitarian reformers of 1832–6, so entirely ignored. But however virtuous or wise may be a principle of public or private action, its survival as the ostensible method of achieving a desired result, *after that principle has ceased to be applicable or adequate to the circumstances of the time*, undermines the very foundations of personal conduct and social organization.

We cannot estimate how far, in previous centuries, the principle of obligatory personal service, nearly always gratuitous, had ever proved sufficient for contemporary needs. What is clear from our researches into eighteenth-century Local Government is that, when certain conditions ceased to prevail, the principle became ineffective. In order to be fulfilled, the duties had to be accepted, as a matter of course, by the great majority of those on whom they were imposed; and supported by the public opinion of the community in which they lived. The services to be rendered had not only to be within the capacity of the ordinary citizen, but also consistent with his earning his livelihood and living his normal life. In short, the obligations had to be customary, limited in extent and unspecialized in character. In many a rural Manor and secluded Parish these conditions were maintained right down to the beginning of the nineteenth century. The little group of freeholders or copyholders, and 'principal inhabitants', continued to fill, with integrity and sufficient skill, all the offices requisite for the life of the small and stationary community. Among these neighbours, each cultivating his agricultural holding or using the common land, or serving, like his forefathers, as village innkeeper or blacksmith, as indoor apprentice or farm-servant, the group-spirit was highly developed. The official relationships among the parties concerned were inextricably interwoven with the economic relationships among the same individuals in their private capacities. The Justice of the Peace was probably himself the Lord of the Manor; his tenants constituted the Leet Jury, presenting nuisances and declaring the customs of the Manor, and they individually served in rotation in all the Parish offices;

they themselves were the employers of the labourers whose poverty they from time to time relieved out of the Poor Rate; and even the clergyman, who was in many respects the most independent person in the village, often owed his position to the squire, let his glebe to the Churchwarden, bargained with the Overseer as to the rates on his tithes, and drew these tithes from every occupier of land in the Parish. Hence, though there might be grumbling, there could be no effective resistance to the action of the governing group. On the other hand, though there were frequently no minutes, and certainly no printed accounts and no newspaper reporters, the persons who did the work and paid the exiguous rates themselves controlled every item of expenditure and knew everything that was going on. Flagrant acts of dishonesty were difficult, and the public approval or blame of the whole village was a real power. But with the increase of trade and population from the close of the seventeenth century, with the dislocation of economic ties, with the rapid transformation of rural districts into busy urban centres entailing new technical services, all the conditions that had made practicable the principle of obligatory, gratuitous and rotational service were swept away, to be replaced by conditions transforming the ancient functions of the old offices into so many opportunities for evasion, peculation and oppression. Round about the City of London, in the unincorporated mining and manufacturing districts of the Northern and Midland Counties, and even within the walls of some of the old-world Municipalities, the new industry and the unaccustomed development of trade were bringing great aggregations of population into ancient Parishes. Here the economic and social relations, which built up the Manor and the Parish, as organs of the 'government by consent' of stable social and economic groups, either had never existed or were in process of rapid disintegration. The powerful tie of landlord and tenant or employer and wage-earner; the strong but intangible link of family relationship or inherited social status, uniting the squire with the clergyman, the farmer with the handicraftsman and labourer, and all these with each other, no longer supplemented the bare legal relationships between the Lord of the Manor and his tenants, the Justice of the Peace and the Overseer, the Incumbent and the People's Churchwarden, the Parish Officers and the Parish ratepayers. The Manor Courts were ceasing to be held, their functions being more and more assumed by the Justices, the Parish Officers and the Vestries. The clergyman of the Parish, often assumed to be the proper chairman of the Vestry, was frequently an absentee, having no other secular or religious connexion with his parishioners than the delegated exaction of his annual tithes and dues. The Justice of the Peace, whose co-operation was the corner-stone of Parish government, without whose signature no Overseer could be appointed, no accounts passed, nor any Poor Rate collected, might be a County magnate, living far away from the new industrial district; or what was worse, a newly enriched tradesman with merely commercial traditions, who had, for personal ends, intrigued himself into the Commission of the Peace. Nor was the failure of supervision of Parish government by the upper classes compensated for, in the vast majority of instances, by any increased watchfulness on the part of the common citizens. The inhabitants of these new industrial districts were unknown to each other; many, as newcomers, were uninterested in the local affairs and unacquainted with the local customs. The time, place and method of appointment of the Parish Officers, such as the Overseers, the Constable and the Surveyor of Highways, together with their powers and functions, were, as far as these uninstructed and indifferent citizens were concerned, shrouded in mystery. Respectable householders might find themselves compelled to undertake an onerous duty against their will by the fact of their names coming next on some list of which they had never heard, or merely because they had been 'presented' by the Vestry or by the previous occupant of the office, either to the Justices or to a surviving Court Leet. When such persons found themselves appointed to act as Constable or Surveyor, Overseer or Churchwarden, they usually did their utmost to escape service. 'The imposition of the office' of Constable, writes Daniel Defoe in 1714, 'is an insupportable hardship; it takes up so much of a man's time that his own affairs are frequently totally neglected, too often to his ruin. Yet there is neither profit nor pleasure therein.'[1] 'It is well known,' reports a Poor Law Commissioner in 1833, 'that when any person who has received a good education, and whose habits are those of a gentleman, settles in a Parish, one of his first objects is to endeavour to exempt himself

[1] *Parochial Tyranny*, by Andrew Moreton (Daniel Defoe), p. 17; *The Parish and the County*, p. 62.

from Parish office.'[1] When it is remembered that it was just in these new industrial districts, or in the still denser aggregations of the Metropolitan area, that the public business of the Parish was becoming every day more complicated and difficult; that the mere number of the paupers was becoming overwhelming; that new buildings of diverse kinds were springing up on all sides; that paving, cleansing, lighting and watching were alike wanting; that the crowding together of tens of thousands of poverty-stricken persons was creating unspeakable nuisances; and that the amount of the rates levied on the inhabitants was at the same time doubling and trebling, it will be easily understood why, in one district after another, the situation became intolerable.

It was not merely that, in these areas, a large part of the public revenue came to be levied in the invidious form of fines exacted from those who wished to buy exemption from the performance of public duties. The abandonment of the offices of the Parish and Manor by all the inhabitants of education, social position or independent means, left these offices to be filled by anyone who sought them as opportunities for making illicit gains. There came to be an almost universal prevalence of perquisites, which might extend from frequent feasts and a total exemption from the payment of rates, up to the most extensive jobbery in supplying the Parish or the Borough with goods at exorbitant prices, and unlimited peculation at the

[1] Communication from a J.P. in Codd's Report, p. 53 of Appendix A of First Report of Poor Law Inquiry Commissioners, 1834; *The Parish and the County*, p. 62.

expense either of terrified inhabitants or of the public funds. In our chapters on 'The Uncontrolled Parish Officers' and 'The Rule of the Boss', we have given detailed examples, typical of a large part of the new England that was growing up in the Northern and Midland Counties, in the ports and the great Metropolitan area, of peculation, extortion and corruption, carried to an extent, continued over terms of years and enjoying an impunity today almost incredible.[1]

But even if men of integrity and public spirit had continued to come forward to fill the old offices of the Manor and the Parish; even if the average citizen had been exact and punctilious in the fulfilment of his accustomed obligations, in the avoidance of nuisances and in performance of Statute Duty, the very change in environment had rendered such personal services wholly unequal to the tasks by which they were faced. Here it was the nature and extent of the obligation itself that was inadequate. The assumption on which universal and gratuitous personal service had always rested was that of a substantially unaltered obligation year after year. The principle was devised for a stable and unchanging community. There was no provision for any new services that might be called for by altered circumstances. The common obligation of the landowners to maintain the sewers did not extend to making a new sewer; that of the County to maintain a bridge carried with it neither duty nor power to construct a new bridge, however urgent might be the need. Whatever might be the growing throng or traffic on the

[1] *The Parish and the County*, pp. 61–90.

highways, no Parish could lawfully make a new thoroughfare, or even raise a footway to a bridleway, or a bridleway to a cartway. It was no part of the obligation of the Parish or of the individual parishioners to transform a muddy country lane, along which a free passage was just possible, into the widened and straightened and artificially prepared road surface that the new traffic required; and even if the new thoroughfare got constructed, nothing more technically skilled or scientifically expert could be required from the Parish in the way of maintenance than could be supplied by the untrained and unspecialized innkeeper or farmer who accepted a year's unpaid service as Surveyor of Highways, directing the temporarily conscripted labour of the crowd of farm-servants and other cottagers who were periodically called out to do Statute Duty on the roads. Even where the character of the required service remained unchanged, its very growth in magnitude took it outside the capacity of the temporarily serving unpaid Parish officer. It was one thing to make the asscssment and collect the rates in a Parish of only a few dozen ratepayers, all of whom were personal acquaintances. It became quite another matter to make the assessment in a crowded Lancashire town, filled with mills and warehouses, shops and foundries of divers kinds; and to collect the rates from thousands of occupiers, many of them merely transient residents.

Vocational Organization as the very Basis of Government

There was another principle behind the local institutions of the seventeenth and eighteenth centuries, one which had become, through senility, a factor of disorganization and demoralization, namely, the acceptance of vocational or occupational organization as a basis of government. At the close of the seventeenth century governmental authority was frequently vested in a group, a company or a corporation associated for some production or supply of services or commodities. The Church, the Universities, the Inns of Court, the College of Physicians, the Company of Surgeons or the Society of Apothecaries could, it seemed, each exercise far-extending authority in connexion with the service that its members rendered to the community as a means of livelihood. Such chartered incorporations as the East India Company, the New River Company, the Bank of England and the various national companies for colonial and foreign trade, or for mining or manufacture, could receive analogous powers.[1] A like association of authority over non-members with economic function and vocational organization can be traced in some, at least, of the local institutions to which we have been referring. The Manorial Court, in its aspect of Court Baron (as distinguished from that of Court Leet, which was a King's Court) was essentially the organ, not of the citizens as such, or of the inhabitants as a whole, but of the particular group of owners or tenants of agricultural land within the Manor—that is to say, notwithstanding

[1] 'In the earlier part of the seventeenth century', writes Dr. Cunningham, 'it appeared to be assumed that the organization of trade by persons who were concerned in it was essential' (*The Growth of English Industry and Commerce in Modern Times,* by Dr. W. Cunningham, 1900, p. 284).

the feudal autocracy that formed its other side, it belonged, like the colleges and companies, to the genus of Associations of Producers. This explains why the typical officers of Local Government in the Manor were the Herdsman, the Common Driver, the Pigringer, the Hayward, and the Pinder or Pound Keeper. This it was that inspired the 'customs' of the Manor, and dictated the elaborate regulation of the common field agriculture, which, in the example of the Manor of Great Tew, occupied so much of the time of the Lord's Court. The same spirit is seen in the clinging of the Freemen of Alnwick or Berwick, Coventry or Newcastle-on-Tyne, to their chartered monopoly of the Town Moor, the Lammas Lands, or the 'Meadows and Stints'. The student of other species of vocational or occupational organization will not be surprised to find the 'Homage' resenting both the intrusion of 'foreigners' into the Manor, and the invasion of the commons by 'landless residents'. The same spirit led, in many a Manor or Manorial Borough, to the exaction of tolls and dues in the market and at the landing-stage exclusively from those who had not been admitted as tenants of the Manor; and sometimes, even in unincorporated villages, induced the Reeve, as representative of the Homage, to charge a fee to such 'foreigners' for the privilege of opening a shop. It was, we suggest, the fact that the Court Baron had the attributes that belong to an Association of Producers which caused it, as is apparent in our account of the Manorial Boroughs, to develop into a close body, renewing itself by co-option, from which the unprivileged inhabitant found himself automatically excluded. But although nearly every Borough retained, even as late as the seventeenth century, at least a remnant of interest in agriculture, most of these urban centres had become, by that time, predominantly communities of traders, whether master-craftsmen, retail shopkeepers or dealers of one sort or another, together with their journeymen, apprentices or other wage-earning assistants. Thus, the Association of Producers in agriculture had, in the Manorial Boroughs, become gradually transformed into an Association of Producers concerned rather with trade and manufacture. This transformation was reflected in the corporate officers and the corporate jurisdictions, involving the appointment of Ale-conners, Fish and Flesh Tasters, and Leather Searchers and Sealers. To the control of the common agriculture there was added a control of the common trading. When we pass from the Manorial Boroughs to the couple of hundred Municipal Corporations, creating their own Justices of the Peace, holding their own civil and criminal Courts, sometimes appointing their own Sheriffs, and in one case even having its own Lieutenancy, independent of the King's appointment, we find this independence frequently intertwined with (and, as some have suggested, usually rooted in, if not arising from) a varying assortment of Merchant or Craft Gilds or Companies, all of them originally Associations of Producers, and basing their membership, not, as in the Manor and the Manorial Borough, on their common interest as agriculturists, but on their common interest in some branch of trade or manufacture. We need not here consider such vexed questions as the exact relation of the Merchant Gild, so frequent in the thirteenth century, on the one hand to the Municipal Corporation itself, and on the other to the Craft Gilds of the fifteenth century; or the varying degrees of independent authority to be attributed, respectively, to the orders and by-laws made by the Craft Gilds for their own trades, of the regulations respecting artificers made by the Municipal Corporation itself, and of the provisions of the Elizabethan Statute of Apprentices, under which, in fact, the eighteenth-century Town Council usually preferred to take proceedings against non-Freemen. What emerges from our analysis of these manorial and municipal exceptions from the common rule of the government of the County by the King's Lieutenant and the King's Justices, is the fact that practically all the regulative activities of these organs of independent authority seem to be connected, at least by traditional origin, not with the common interests of all men as citizens and consumers, but with the particular interests of the members as locally privileged groups of agriculturists, traders or manufacturers. It is to this primordial conception of an organization based on common interests as producers, not wherever they resided but only within a delimited area, that we trace the various forms of trade monopoly which characterize alike the Craft Gild and Trade Company, the Manorial Borough and the Municipal Corporation, from the prohibition of the letting of crofts, 'stints', boats, market-stalls, shops or houses to 'foreigners', up to the restriction of trades to Freemen, or to the sons or apprentices of Freemen, being also members of a particular Gild or Company. We see the same principle in the habitual secrecy of the proceedings of the Municipal Corporation as of the Gild; the same notion of its transactions being those of a voluntary and private association; the same abhorrence of any external supervision or control; the same inability to recognize any justification for the demand for accounts, let alone an outside audit. We see the same idea in the exemption of Freemen from the tolls and dues levied by the Municipal Corporation (which was simply themselves), or if Freemen paid anything at all, the mulcting of non-Freemen in higher charges. A Municipal Corporation, feeling itself merely a group of privileged persons, inevitably considered its market or its port, like its commons or its charitable endowments, as belonging morally as well as legally to its members, and to its members exclusively. And this Association of Producers retained, to the last, certain characteristics of an essentially voluntary fellowship. Alike in the Municipal Corporation and in the Gild or Company, a new member could enter only by the consent of the existing corporate body, just as a new tenant of the Manor had to be formally admitted by the Homage at the Lord's Court. Any member could be, for sufficient reason and with due formalities, expelled from the Corporation at its discretion. The Municipal Corporation, like the Gild, was thus, in fact, not only an Association of Producers, but also an association voluntarily recruited at the option of the existing members, who felt that they had a privilege to bestow. It was therefore at all times an association falling far short of universality; and in no way identified particularly with mere inhabitancy or residence, or, as would now be said, with local citizenship.[1]

The Undermining of the Vocational Basis of Local Institutions

At the close of the seventeenth century, when the National Government, as we have explained, ceased to give any attention to, or to take any interest in, the development of local institutions, the Manor, the Manorial Borough and the Municipal Corporation were already in an advanced stage of constitutional decay. Their functions in their character of Associations of Producers were already, for the most part, obsolescent, owing to the upgrowth of new and rival forms of organization, alike in agriculture, in commerce and in manufacture, entailing a divorce continuously more complete and more universal, of the mass of the workers from all participation in the ownership and direction of the instruments of production. With the rapidly increasing statutory enclosures, and the still more revolutionary introduction of the factory, the machine-industry and the steam engine, and the universal improvement in the means of communication, this continuous retreat of the independent

[1] It would, we think, be far-fetched to emphasize traces of vocational organization in the County or Parish government. But it is worth noting that the Justices belonged originally all to one class, that of owners of agricultural land, with which their connexion was much more than that of receivers of rent. They were, in fact, the directors of agricultural enterprise. And though the Parish organization, resting as it did, from at least the fourteenth century, on the meeting of the 'principal inhabitants' in Vestry assembled, was distinctively communal in character, the members, in practice, were usually all agriculturists.

peasant cultivator and the master craftsman became, before the end of the eighteenth century, nearly everywhere a disastrous rout. The Manorial Courts, dependent on the continuance of groups of freeholders or copy-holders as agricultural producers, were one by one silently discontinued as organs of local administration. In such urban areas as Birmingham and Manchester, they lingered in distorted form as the framework of an attenuated Local Government, based on customary obligation, but divorced from all contact with the bulk of the residents, and becoming increasingly subordinated to the meeting of the inhabitants in Vestry assembled, or to the County Justices of the Peace. Much the same decay fell on the great majority of the Municipal Corporations, which found that their immemorial connexion with the privileges of the Freemen, or with the Gilds or Companies, inevitably entailed an ever-increasing separation from the great body of the inhabitants. Only in a few cases, where the Freemen continued to be not so far behind the whole number of householders; and notably in the City of London, where the Livery Companies, though losing their connexion with the vocations of which they bore the names, were wealthy property owners, their leading members continuing to be individually associated with commerce, do we see the members of the Corporation becoming, not indeed a vocational, but, in effect, a ratepayers' Democracy. And even in the City of London, the Companies themselves, like nearly all the Municipal Corporations elsewhere, shrank up into limited groups of privileged persons, recruiting themselves by co-option, and having an ever-dwindling community of interest with the inhabitants at large. It was this progressive decay of the vocational basis of municipal structure that caused the vast majority of Municipal Corporations to become, from the standpoint of Local Government, little more than an expedient for recruiting a local bench of magistrates, who, within the privileged area, exercised much of the authority of the County Justices.

The Principle of 'Self-election' or Co-option

To the modern student, who might expect to find in the eighteenth century the beginning of the political Democracy of the nineteenth, it is a shock to discover that by far the most widely approved constitution for local institutions, right down to the early decades of the nineteenth century, was the distinctively oligarchical structure of a close body recruiting itself by co-option. Among the Local Authorities of this period the meeting of inhabitants in Vestry assembled was the only one in which anything like a communal Democracy can be seen, or any germ of a government of the people, by the people, and for the people. And yet, even in Parish organization, the Select Vestry crops up sporadically over nearly all parts of England and becomes actually the common form in the cities of London, Westminster and Bristol, and in Northumberland and Durham. Sometimes this Select Vestry, styled indifferently 'the Gentlemen of the Four and Twenty', 'the Company of the Twelve', 'the Masters of the Parish', or 'the Kirk Masters', claimed to derive its authority from a custom 'whereof the memory of man runneth not to the contrary'. But on examination of the records we found this immemorial custom sometimes entangled in the occupation or tenure of particular husbandries or farms, probably inherited from some Manorial organization; in other cases we found it originating in a resolution of the Open Vestry in the sixteenth or seventeenth century, whereby 'it is agreed by the consent of the whole Parish, to elect and choose out of the same, twelve men to order and define all common causes pertaining to the church, as shall appertain to the profit and commodity of the same, without molestation or troubling of the rest of the common people'.[1] But for the most part these Select Vestries were deliberately brought into being, expressly in order to exclude the common folk, not by local agreement, but by bishops' faculty; or, in the course of the eighteenth or the first decades of the nineteenth century, by Local Act. Even as late as 1819 the redoubtable Thomas Rhodes succeeded in getting an Act completely extinguishing the turbulent Open Vestry of St. Pancras (which he had for twenty years been stripping of its powers), expressly forbidding any such body to meet for the future; and transferring all the property and the powers, both of the Vestry and of the Directors of the Poor, to a Select Vestry of persons named in the Act, and entitled to fill up vacancies by co-option.

When we turn from Parish government to the Municipal Corporations, we find the great majority of these, amounting to three-quarters of the whole,

[1] *Churchwardens' Accounts of Pittington and other Parishes in the Diocese of Durham from 1580 to 1700* (Surtees Society, vol. lxxxiv, 1888), p. 12; *The Parish and the County*, pp. 184–5.

governed each by a close body. This body, whether styled Court of Common Council, Court of Aldermen, or the Mayor and Commonalty, itself elected the Mayor or other head of the Corporation, and filled vacancies in its ranks by simple co-option. In these cases, even if there existed also a large body of members of the Corporation, styled Freemen, who were recruited by apprenticeship, patrimony or purchase, they found themselves excluded from the government of the Corporation, ranking merely as humble participants in some of its profitable privileges, such as freedom from toll, eligibility for charities, and right to 'stint of common'.[1] This kind of government it was that the Royal Commission of 1835 stigmatized as 'the Corporation System', and assumed to be representative of all the Municipal Corporations. We need not here inquire whether the close body derived its authority from the original or from an amending charter; or merely from the existence or presumption of a by-law of the Corporation itself. 'The Twenty-Four', recites one of these municipal by-laws, 'shall be instead of the whole commonalty, and no other of the commonalty to intermeddle upon pain of five pounds'.[2] It is significant

[1] The Law Courts seem willingly to have accepted mere usage as warranting this exclusion, and even to have been prepared to presume from usage within living memory the existence of a by-law 'restraining to a select body the right of election of the principal corporators, though vested by the ancient constitution in the popular assembly' (*The Law of Municipal Corporations*, by J. W. Willcock, 1828, p. 8; *The Manor and the Borough*, p. 274).

[2] MS. Minutes, Corporation of Romney Marsh (Kent), 1604; *The Manor and the Borough*, p. 361. A lesser revolution might be effected by a by-law relating to the election or qualifications of the Common Council, the Aldermen, or the

of the state of public opinion, as late as 1808, that we find 'the public committee of Manchester citizens', which then headed the reform movement in this unincorporated town, expressing the desire that Manchester should be endowed with municipal institutions similar to those of Leeds, 'self-elect' though these were. 'We conceive', they declared, 'that a permanent body of guardians of the peace, clothed with the authority of magistracy, would here, as in other places, be the natural guardian of all interior public interests, able to conduct them with uniformity and consistency, and ready at all times for the immediate prevention or correction of abuses, and might represent the inhabitants in all their external relations with a character and dignity becoming the largest provincial community in the United Kingdom.'[1]

Even among the County Justices, who gloried in being the directly appointed officers of the King, we find the principle of co-option coming in at the beginning of the nineteenth century, if not earlier. As we have described, the scandalous breakdown of the Middlesex Bench was attributed to the carelessness and favouritism which permitted the appointment, in the name of the Crown, of 'men of low degree', who became the notorious 'Basket Justices' or 'Trading Justices', shamelessly using their office for corrupt, oppressive and even fraudulent purposes. Many are the complaints by the Justices themselves, to be found

Justices of the Peace; usually of a restrictive tendency, either in transferring the right to appoint to a smaller body, or limiting the persons eligible for appointment.

[1] *Report of Committee to obtain Reforms* (Manchester, 1808): *The Manor and the Borough*, vol. ii, p. 422.

not only in Quarter Sessions records, but also in the 'Magistrates' Book' in the Home Office archives, of 'gross misconduct and unfitness' and of 'scandalous corruption and extortion' among these unworthy nominees of the Crown. With the upgrowth of the movement for 'the reformation of morals and manners', initiated by the Royal Proclamation against vice and immorality, issued early in 1787 at the instance of Wilberforce, the County Justices began to insist on nominating their colleagues and successors. The reader will recall the case of the Merionethshire County Magistrates who, in 1833, actually 'went on strike' for a time, in their resentment of the appointment of a wealthy local landowner, because he had, within their recollection, kept a retail shop, and still belonged to 'the Methodists'. They objected to this individual, we are told, not so much on account of religious differences, which might possibly have been overlooked, but because his origin, his education, his connexions, his early habits, occupations and station were not such as could entitle him to be the familiar associate of gentlemen. 'The refusal of the County Magistrates', declared an exceptionally Conservative member of the Municipal Corporations Commission, 'to act with a man who has been a grocer and is a Methodist is the dictate of genuine patriotism: the spirit of aristocracy in the County magistracy is the salt which alone saves the whole mass from inevitable corruption.'[1] Under the influence of this spirit of mingled reformation and exclusiveness, the County benches came to be, at any

[1] *Report on Certain Boroughs*, T. S. Hogg (H.C. No. 686 of 1838, p. 5); *The Parish and the County*, p. 385.

rate from the early part of the nineteenth century, normally recruited by what practically amounted to co-option, the Lord Chancellor habitually accepting the nominations of the Lord Lieutenant, and the latter expressing the views and desires of the active Justices. The result was, notwithstanding a rapid and continuous increase in the number of Justices during the first few decades of the nineteenth century, a quickly developing homogeneity among them in social status and political opinions.

A conclusive demonstration of the common acceptance during the eighteenth century of the oligarchical principle of self-election or co-option is afforded by its deliberate adoption for the great majority of Statutory Bodies for Special Purposes described in the present volume. The most numerous of all these bodies, the Turnpike Trusts, consisted, from first to last, of persons named in the Act, who were always empowered to continue the existence of the Trust by co-opting other persons to fill vacancies. The more important, though far less numerous, Improvement Commissions exhibited more variety in their constitutional structure. But throughout the eighteenth century, the majority of these bodies were constituted as sets of named persons, together with some ex-officio members, the body as a whole always recruiting itself by co-option. It is only in the early decades of the nineteenth century that we find the amending Acts tentatively introducing the element of election by the ratepayers. And though in the Incorporated Guardians of the Poor the principle of elections was, even in the earliest examples, usually introduced to some extent, amid ex-officio members and others designated by status or named in the Act, vacancies were usually filled by co-option.

To the political philosopher the principle of co-option or self-election, as the method of recruiting a governing body, has interesting affiliations to other oligarchical constitutions. By their very nature, the non-elective Municipal Corporations were assumed to belong to the same political category as the hereditary monarchy, the House of Lords, the Established Church and the freehold tenure of public office. Had not Edmund Burke himself declared that 'Corporations, which have a perpetual succession and an hereditary *noblesse*, who themselves exist by succession, are the true guardians of monarchical succession'?[1] Thus it was not without reason that the 'Corporation System' found in the House of Lords of 1835 its last and most vehement supporters. More interesting to the philosopher of today is the historical connexion of the principle of co-option with the two other contemporary features that we have described—the common obligation to hold public office and vocational organization as the basis of government. Thus, we find in the records of many Parishes that the officers for the time being, whether Church-wardens, Overseers, Surveyors or Constables, habitually nominated their successors. It was the serving officers who were keenest to get other substantial inhabitants to take over their onerous and troublesome duties. It was, in fact, the little meeting of Parish Officers, with their empirical practice of

[1] Burke to the Chevalier de Rivarol, in 1791, in *Correspondence of Edmund Burke*, by Earl Fitzwilliam and Sir R. Bourke, 1844, vol. iii, p. 212; *The Manor and the Borough*, p. 703.

choosing their successors, that frequently constituted itself, by one or other instrument, a Select Vestry for all purposes of Parish organization, to the exclusion of all the other inhabitants. The same notion that those who do the work at any given time are the best judges of those who should do it in the future, is deeply rooted in all vocational organization, both medieval and modern. There is, however, one significant difference between medieval and modern vocational organization. Prior to the advent of the Trade Union Movement it was taken for granted that there must necessarily be, within each vocation, one or more superior grades—an inner oligarchy that would, whatever its own method of appointment, exercise some sort of jurisdiction over the humbler members. Bishops in the church, Benchers in the legal profession, Fellows in the Royal Colleges of Physicians and Surgeons, the master-craftsmen in the gilds, all alike claimed to hold the gateway through which were admitted into the vocation the junior or inferior grades of priests, barristers, licentiates or journeymen: in a word, the great body of practitioners of the profession or craft. Thus, if to the principle of vocational organization be added the conception of graded status, there emerge in full view the 'Corporation System' and the 'Select Vestry System', which were swept away by the democratic reforms of 1830–5.

The Virtues and Vices of the Oligarchical Principle of Co-option or Self-election

Is it possible to summarise the effects, good and evil, which this oligarchical principle of renewal by co-option had on the administration and procedure of local institutions? For it so happens that this very period of history gives us a unique opportunity of distinguishing the virtues and vices of this form of government in comparison with other and more democratic constitutions. Alike in Parish and Municipal government, and in the Statutory Authorities for Special Purposes, there is an opportunity of comparing Authorities recruited by co-option and Authorities established and renewed by popular election, either by the inhabitants at large, or by the ratepayers as such, or at least by large bodies of manual-working Freemen. In Parish government the oligarchical form was the exception, whilst the more democratic practice became increasingly the rule. In municipal government, on the other hand, democratic practice was exceptional and the oligarchical form was the rule; whilst in the Statutory Authorities for Special Purposes we not infrequently see effected by Local Acts a sudden transformation of an oligarchical into an elective constitution.

The first conclusion to be deduced from this extensive and varied material may seem paradoxical: it is that close bodies display not only the utmost variety among themselves; but also even greater extremes than may be found among bodies of any other constitution. Some are more timid, others more audacious, in the use of their multifarious powers than democracies of inhabitants, democracies of ratepayers or democracies of Freemen. Some are seen to sink to the lowest depths of maladministration and venality, whilst a few reach a level of efficiency and honesty not attained during these hundred and fifty years by any other parochial or municipal authorities. Let us take first the Parish organization. 'These Select Vestries', said a blunt critic of 1828, 'are a focus of jobbing; the draper supplies the blankets and linen; the carpenter finds the church pews constantly out of repair; the painter's brushes are never dry; the plumber is always busy with his solder; and thus the public money is plundered and consumed.'[1] 'Select Vestries are select companies of rogues',[2] said another, seventy years before—a verdict undoubtedly true of the majority of these close bodies. But there were one or two exceptions. The Select Vestry of St. George's, Hanover Square, for instance, as it seems to us, attained a higher level of efficiency and integrity than any other contemporary Local Authority, and enjoyed a remarkable freedom from adverse criticism of either policy or administration. The minutes and other records of this Parish, from 1725 onward, reveal the Select Vestry as a little knot of public-spirited peers and gentry who governed their great and wealthy Parish with consistent honesty, and, relatively to the standards of the time, with exceptional efficiency. In later years this Select Vestry, strengthened by successive Local Acts, paved, watched and lighted the streets and squares; carried out a certain amount of scavenging and suppressed nuisances; systematized the assessment and collection of the rates, and put a stop to illegal exemptions; and, in the administration of the Poor Law, voluntarily anticipated by

[1] *Sunday Times*, 1828, quoted in *Considerations on Select Vestries*, 1828, p. 49; *The Parish and the County*, p. 233.

[2] *The Constitutional*, quoted in *The Select Vestry Justified*, 1754, p. 14; *The Parish and the County*, p. 233.

several years some of the reforms of 1834. No evidence of maladministration was produced against these vestrymen before the House of Commons Select Committee of 1829; and when, in 1832, the inhabitants had the opportunity of electing a new Vestry, they contented themselves with unanimously choosing their old governors. Our own impression is that, during the eighteenth century and the first quarter of the nineteenth, St. George's, Hanover Square, was, under its Select Vestry, by far the best-governed Parish in the Metropolitan area.

Much the same may be said of the Municipal Corporations. No one who studies the records of such close corporations as those of Leicester and Coventry, together with case after case in a hundred other Boroughs, can doubt the substantial accuracy of the condemnation of many of these oligarchies by the Municipal Corporation Commissioners in 1835, as guilty of 'mismanagement of the corporate property of the most glaring kind', the 'alienation in fee of the corporate property to individual corporators', the 'execution of long leases for nominal consideration', the 'voting of salaries to sinecure, unnecessary or overpaid officers', the devotion of their income to 'entertainments of the Common Council and their friends', the misappropriation of trust funds 'to gain or reward votes both at the Municipal and Parliamentary elections'; and, in short, of an almost unparalleled neglect of public duty and failure to promote the well-being of their respective Boroughs. On the other hand, there were a few Boroughs, no less oligarchical in their constitutions, such as Penzance at one end of the Kingdom and Wisbech at the other, which were reported as free from all the vices discovered among their neighbours—a verdict which our own closer investigation of the records has completely confirmed. Moreover, the greatest of all the provincial municipalities, that of Liverpool, whilst maintaining its rigidly exclusive oligarchy, showed itself, generation after generation, markedly superior in energy, dignity, integrity and public spirit to any other Municipal Corporation in the land, not excluding the 'ratepayers' democracy' of the City of London itself. Its Bench of Aldermen discharged gratuitously the whole burdensome duty of magistracy for the town and docks; governed the largest provincial police force of the Kingdom in a way to give satisfaction to the inhabitants; and kept the five local prisons in a state of relatively high efficiency. The close body of the Mayor and two Bailiffs and thirty or forty Aldermen or Common Councilmen, recruiting itself exclusively by co-option, not only gave to the town its magistrates, but also acted itself as Lord of the Manor and owned in fee simple a large portion of the land; it governed the port; it erected markets, warehouses and public baths; it provided weigh-bridges and a chain-cable testing-machine for common use; it spent large sums on widening the streets and generally improving the town; it lavished money on the building and endowment of new churches, and latterly it established and maintained at its own expense extensive free schools. In any emergency the Corporation came forward to serve the interests of its important commercial community. More than once, during the eighteenth century, from 1715 down to 1803, it undertook the defence of the port, raising regiments, erecting batteries and equipping gunboats at its own expense. In the commercial crisis which occurred at the sudden declaration of war in 1793, when banks and business firms were failing on all sides, the Liverpool Corporation took the boldest financial step recorded in the annals of English Local Government. It first tried to borrow £100,000 from the Bank of England, with which to uphold the credit of the principal Liverpool houses; and when the loan was not forthcoming, it promptly obtained power from Parliament to issue, up to a maximum of £300,000, its own promissory notes payable to bearer, which were accepted as currency. In this way it advanced no less than £140,000 to the local merchants, on the security of their temporarily unsaleable goods, to enable them to meet their engagements; with the result that the panic was stayed, failures were prevented, and the whole sum, with interest, was within three years recovered without loss. It remains to be added that this self-elected Corporation made way for the representative body with unusual dignity. Unlike all the other wealthy Municipal Corporations, the Liverpool Town Council refused to oppose its own abolition. At a special meeting summoned to consider the Municipal Corporations Bill, we find it resolving 'That this Council, conscious of having always discharged the important duties devolved upon it as the governing body of this Corporation with the utmost desire for the welfare and advantage of the Town of Liverpool, does not feel itself called upon to offer any opposition to the principle of the measure brought into the House of Commons, so far as relates to the removal of the members of this Council, and the substitution of another body by a different mode of election for the future management of the corporate estate, but that the same should be left to such determination as Parliament may think fit regarding it.'[1]

The paradox of so extreme a divergence in administrative results among a group of Local Authorities practically identical in the form of their government is capable of explanation. The working of the principle of co-option depends in the main on two conditions: first the characteristics of the persons who are in office at the start, and secondly the existence, within the circle of eligibility, of persons of like character. The subsequent development of all these bodies is governed by the rule that 'like attacts like'. In the majority of urban Parishes in which a Select Vestry was started, this close body fell, from the outset, into the hands of the small shopkeepers, master-craftsmen and builders, to whom the opportunities for eating, drinking and making excursions at the public expense, and the larger gains of extending their little businesses by Parish work, offered an irresistible temptation. The Select Vestry came more and more to attract the less scrupulous and to repel the more refined members of this class, whilst the filling of vacancies by co-option tended inevitably to make the whole body homogeneous in its low standard of public morality. 'As the old ones drop off', Defoe had remarked in 1714, 'they are sure to choose none in their room but those whom

[1] MS. Minutes, Corporation of Liverpool, at special meeting to consider the Municipal Corporations Bill, 17 June 1835; *The Manor and the Borough*, pp. 490–1.

they have marked for their purpose beforehand; so rogue succeeds rogue, and the same scene of villainy is still carried on, to the terror of the poor parishioners.'[1] On the other hand, in St. George's, Hanover Square, the Select Vestry was composed, from the start, exclusively of persons unconnected with trade, and moving in a different sphere. The 'noblemen and gentlemen' of the West End squares were, as a class, quite as unscrupulous as the shopkeepers of Spitalfields, in obtaining pay without work, at the public expense. But the opportunities of this class for plunder and jobbery—for the most scandalous public sinecures and pensions, and bribes from the secret-service money dispensed at the Treasury—lay in another direction. Feeding and driving in carriages at the Parish expense was no temptation to them. The supply of groceries to the workhouse, or the repainting of the Parish church, offered them no chance of profit. Hence this Select Vestry attached to itself, not the unscrupulous and avaricious members of its class, but those who took an interest as owners, occupiers, or philanthropists, in the good government of their parish. And here, equally, the practice of co-option tended constantly to a homogeneity of motives and manners and morals.

It is needless to trace the same principle of 'like attracting like' in the degeneration of the majority of the Municipal Corporations. In those few municipalities in which, for some reason, the Corporation

[1] *Parochial Tyranny, or the Housekeeper's Complaint against the Insupportable Exactions and Partial Assessments of Select Vestries, etc.*, by Andrew Moreton (i.e. Daniel Defoe), 1714 (?), p. 10; *The Parish and the County*, p. 245.

business continued in the hands of a close body of old established and reputable resident families (in the case of Liverpool, substantial merchants and shopkeepers; in the cases of Penzance and Wisbech, hereditary fishermen, master-craftsmen and yeomen cultivators), the municipal business was carried on by successive generations of honourable and public-spirited administrators in the interests of the whole community. But with the surging of new populations in some Boroughs, and with the progressive exclusion or withdrawal of the principal inhabitants or more respectable citizens from the close bodies of other Corporations, we see these oligarchies more and more recruiting themselves from inferior strata. When once the deterioration began the disease grew rapidly worse, without possibility of recovery. The close body made up of venal corrupt and incompetent men continued to recruit itself from men of like character, and became a source of infection to all who came in contact with it. Such being the tendencies at work, it is not surprising that, whilst one or two close bodies remained superior alike in initiative and honourable conduct to any of their contemporaries, the vast majority fell even below the mediocre standard of administrative efficiency and pecuniary honesty that prevailed in the open Vestries and democratically controlled municipalities of the eighteenth and early nineteenth centuries.

The Vice of Exclusiveness

There was one vice which even the best of the close bodies manifested, a vice which, as a matter of fact, was eventually more responsible for their undoing than any lapse in administrative capacity or pecuniary honesty. The same law of 'like attracts like', inherent in the device of co-option, caused 'the Gentlemen of the Four-and-Twenty', or 'the Company of the Twelve' of the Select Vestry, and the little oligarchy called the Court of Aldermen, or the Common Council, or the Mayor and the Bailiffs and Commonalty of the Municipal Corporation, vehemently to object to inviting any person to participate in the work of government who did not share their own political and religious views. Already, in 1635, we find it reported to the Star Chamber that the Parish of St. Andrew's, Holborn, had 'a Selected Vestry of twelve persons, grave and ancient inhabitants, men of approved, honest and good discretion, and (*which is ever regarded in their choice*) men that are known to be well addicted to the rites and ceremonies of the Church of England, and no way prone to faction. [1] In Bristol the gross political partisanship of the close Vestries, century after century, was notorious. It was the support which the Metropolitan Close Vestries gave to the Tory and High Church party that, more than anything else, earned for them, during the eighteenth century, the repeated hostile criticism of the Whigs in the House of Commons; the not unbiased accusations of such contemporaries as Oldmixon and Calamy, and the satirical abuse of Daniel Defoe. After the French Revolution these same Close Vestries everywhere formed a wall of resistance to Radicalism against which those who strove for reforms of any kind long beat in vain. In the

[1] MS. Chartae Miscellaneae, vol. vii, p. 57, in Lambeth Palace Library; *The Parish and the County*, p. 242.

Municipal Corporations the vice of exclusiveness had even more sensational results. These oligarchies often controlled large incomes and an indefinite amount of patronage. They provided the bench of magistrates which administered justice, and they controlled such police forces as existed. More important than all, they frequently elected the Members of Parliament. For the most part, this political and religious partisanship, gross and unashamed, was inextricably entangled (as at Coventry and Leicester) with favouritism and bribery, and even oppression of fellow-citizens. The Leicester corporators, it is to be noted, gloried in their religious and political exclusiveness. 'Holding with fervour', they resolved in 1790, 'that conscientious men have the strongest of all possible motives to support and extend their own party, namely, the supposition that they alone are in possession of the truth', they avowedly never 'scrupuled to use their whole influence and authority, whether as magistrates, as landlords, as trustees of charities or as municipal administrators to put their own party into power.'[1] But even without corruption or misappropriation of funds, the very zeal and public spirit of an oligarchical Municipal Corporation might make its exclusiveness more offensive. The Mayor, Bailiffs, and Burgesses of Liverpool would probably have aroused less hostility among the powerful groups of dissenters rising to wealth in this flourishing port if they had merely wasted the corporate funds on feasting and jaunts, in corrupt leases and contracts, instead of spending the income, not only on docks and

[1] MS. Minutes, Corporation of Leicester, 23 February 1790; *The Manor and the Borough*, vol. ii, pp. 477–9.

street improvements but also in repairing and redecorating old churches, in building new ones, in endowing clergymen, and most obnoxious of all, in maintaining free schools in which the catechism of the Established Church was made the basis of religious instruction. It was true that bribery, licentiousness and corruption disgraced the municipal elections of the so-called municipal democracies of Norwich and Ipswich. But in this pandemonium Whigs and Tories were alike involved; though the majority of citizens, the non Freemen, found themselves excluded from the chance of sharing in the spoils. What was at the time the most powerful and the most complete municipal democracy in the world, the City of London, scandalously neglected its port, its prisons and its police, and spent little or nothing out of its huge income on religion, education, science or art.[1] Yet it was exempted from the iconoclastic Municipal Corporations Act of 1835—an exemption due, not to any purity of administration or freedom from jobbery, but primarily to the fact that it was not a close body, which made it inconvenient for the City to be included in the main Report of the Commissioners. It had, as we have seen, become virtually a ratepayer's democracy, with a long tradition of defiant independence, in the name of the people, of either King or Government. This development into a ratepayers' democracy gave the City of London, notwithstanding the scandalous corruption and extravagance that continued for at least another generation, sufficient political influence to save it from the reform that hardly any 'close' body escaped. Thus, it was not

[1] *The Manor and the Borough*, vol. ii, pp. 690–2.

the administrative inefficiency or the failure in honesty that brought down the local oligarchies, but above all their exclusiveness. Without the prodding of hatred caused by their political and religious partisanship it is doubtful whether there could have arisen in 1830–6 any popular movement for their radical reform.

Freehold Office

Another characteristic feature of the ancient order continued into the eighteenth century; and may, indeed, be found lingering down to our day. This was the permanent, or as it was often expressed, freehold tenure of the older offices. In the Parish, not only the incumbent of the living, whether rector or vicar, but also the immemorial Parish Clerk, once usually in minor orders, held office for life; and were legally entitled to enforce payment of their customary dues and fees of office, irrespective of any particular service rendered. In the County a like tenure was enjoyed by an officer of far greater importance in the local administration, namely, the Clerk of the Peace, who was, in fact, under no control at all. The appointment on the occurrence of a vacancy, was in the hands, not of the Justices in Quarter Sessions, but of the Lord-Lieutenant; who had, however, no power of dismissal from office, and no right to give any instructions as to the performance of the customary duties, for which fees could be exacted. The Clerk of the Peace had an exclusive legal right to perform these duties, and to receive the fees; and these rights he was by statute[1]

[1] 37 Henry VIII. c. 1, sec. 3; 1 William and Mary, c. 21, sec. 4.

authorized to devolve upon a deputy, whom he could appoint at his discretion. The office was, in certain cases, almost openly bought and sold; but more usually, whilst the Clerkship of the Peace was held as a sinecure, the Deputy Clerkship was held, practically as an hereditary possession, by the principal firm of solicitors in the County town, which took the multitudinous fees as part of its profits. Under these circumstances it was natural that the Justices should find it almost impossible to get done any work for which a fee could not be charged. 'For a considerable time past', reports a Committee of the Middlesex Quarter Sessions, 'great inconvenience has been felt for want of due attention in certain departments of the office of the Clerk of the Peace. Public business is often impeded and the time of the magistrates unnecessarily consumed by the irregular attendance of the proper officer, and by the delays occasioned in searching for books and papers which, if found at all, are with much difficulty procured.'[1] When Sir James Graham, then newly elected to Parliament for Carlisle, alarmed at the rapid rise of the County rate, began to overhaul the accounts of the Clerk of the Peace (who ran up his fees by charging, for instance, £7 or £10 for his attendance at each meeting), and demanded a regular checking of the quarterly bills by one or two Justices before they were formally presented to the Court to be passed for payment, he was met by an indignant protest. 'It is a very unpleasant thing', complained the offended official, 'to have one's

[1] Report of Committee on the Records, MS. Minutes, Quarter Sessions, Middlesex, 9 December 1824; *The Parish and the County*, p. 505.

bill handed round for everyone's inspection.'[1] The remuneration of public officers by allowing them to charge fees on all the business that they transacted, went along with the right of property in offices. But it was especially characteristic, as we have mentioned,[2] 'of the system which aimed at making the administration of justice self-supporting". The scandal of the system was that unscrupulous officers, not excluding Justices of the Peace, made the fees yield an income by a perpetual flow of business, which it thus became their interest to promote.

Another ancient office of the County held practically by life-tenure was that of the Coroner, who was, apart from numerous exceptions in particular Liberties or Franchises, elected by the freeholders of the County, had a legal right to perform the customary duties, and could enforce payment of the customary fees. The Coroner was under no one's orders; and although he was nominally subjected to dismissal from office by the Crown by special writ, he was in practice irremovable. For the rest, it must be said that the Lord-Lieutenant and the Justices of the Peace, like almost all nominees of the Crown, were normally appointed for life; and only in the rarest cases, usually connected with political partisanship, were they dismissed. In the Manorial Boroughs and Municipal Corporations, as in the Select Vestries and in nearly all the various Statutory Authorities for Special Purposes, life-office was the rule; and though here and there the Crown

[1] Lonsdale's *Worthies of Cumberland*, 1868, vol. ii, p. 81; *The Parish and the County*, p. 507.

[2] *The Parish and the County*, p. 326.

might, in theory, have a more or less nominal right of removal, the tenure was, in normal times, rightly looked upon as equivalent to freehold.

Now, what was open to objection in this life-tenure in public office, which had once been a matter of course, when public office was so frequently, to use the words of Blackstone, an incorporeal hereditament, was not the security of tenure itself, enjoyed today by all persons exercising judicial functions, and even by the bulk of our Civil Servants, but (in administrative offices) the absence of any control and power of direction; (in all offices) the lack of any practical means of even requiring the due performance of the duties of the position; and, what was specially characteristic of the eighteenth century, the assumption that all those who were selected to fill offices of honour or authority should be owners of property, and, originally, even owners of a particular kind of property, namely, land.

The Property Qualification

Running like a red thread through all the local institutions of the eighteenth century was the assumption that the ownership of property, more particularly landed property, carried with it, not only a necessary qualification for, but even a positive right to carry on, the work of government. 'We may describe feudalism', writes F. W. Maitland, 'as a state of society in which all or a great part of public rights and duties are inextricably interwoven with the tenure of land, in which the whole governmental system—financial, military, judicial—is part of the law of private property. . . . It is utterly impossible to speak of our medieval constitution except in terms of our medieval land law.'[1] It must be admitted that, if we accept this definition, the feudal system was far from being extinct in the England of the eighteenth and early nineteenth centuries. It is needless to recall to the reader the intimate connexion between the ownership of land and the still surviving Courts and officers of the Manor and the Manorial Borough; and the intermingling of the occupation of land with the ecclesiastical and secular constitution of Parish Government. In the foregoing chapters of this volume we have shown how this red thread of property qualification (and, wherever possible, landed property) is an almost universal feature in the constitution of the Statutory Authority for Special Purposes. Far more significant was the fact that the most powerful of all the local institutions of this period, the Commission of the Peace, was based on the landed interest. 'In this Kingdom', writes an indignant pamphleteer of 1748, 'any booby is invested with the ensigns of magistracy, provided he has as many acres of land as are necessary to qualify him under the Act. . . . Thus, they are nominated by dint of estate, or ministerial influence, without any regard to their knowledge, virtue, or integrity. . . . After this manner in every County we have ignorant petty tyrants constituted to lord it over us, instead of honourable, ingenuous, upright, conscientious, learned and judicious magistrates.'[2] Nor can it be said that the practice into which the Crown, during the eighteenth

[1] *The Constitutional History of England*, 1919, pp. 23–24.
[2] Pamphlet of 1748 quoted in *Morning Chronicle*, 3 December 1824; *The Parish and the County*, p. 346.

century, sometimes fell, of appointing men as magistrates without the qualification of good estate, was justified by its results. 'In places inhabited by the scum and dregs of the people and the most profligate class of life, gentlemen of any great figure or fortune', writes a contemporary journalist, 'will not take such drudgery upon them.'[1] Successive Lord Chancellors found themselves, especially in Middlesex, driven to fill the Commission with small professionals and tradesmen who, as it was said, 'had picked up a little knowledge by attending on Special Juries, and thought themselves lawyers'.[2] 'The Justices of Middlesex', said Burke without contradiction in 1780, 'were generally the scum of the earth—carpenters, brickmakers and shoemakers; some of whom were notoriously men of such infamous characters that they were unworthy of any employ whatever, and others so ignorant that they could scarcely write their own names.'[3] Thus we find, up and down the country, but especially in Middlesex (including Westminster and the Tower Hamlets) and the Metropolitan parts of Surrey, a particular type of Justice who, as we have seen, gained, in the documents and literature of the eighteenth century, an infamous notoriety under the appellation of a 'Basket' or 'Trading Justice'. With the improvement in the choice of Justices, and the slowly rising standard of manners and morals, the 'Justice of Mean Degree' had, at the end

[1] *Applebee's Journal*, 19 August 1732, quoted in *Gentleman's Magazine*, August 1732, p. 910; *The Parish and the County*, p. 324.

[2] *Memoirs, etc., of Laetitia Matilda Hawkins*, 1824, vol. i, p. 18; *The Parish and the County*, p. 324.

[3] *Parliamentary History*, 8 May 1780, vol. xxi, p. 592; *The Parish and the County*, p. 325.

of the first quarter of the nineteenth century, been gradually eliminated. Meanwhile the tacit adoption by the Lords-Lieutenant of the principle of co-option, coupled with the real social apprehension and fierce political cleavages that marked the era of the French Revolution, had caused the Rulers of the County to be chosen, more than ever, exclusively from one social class—the landed gentry, who, it must be added, belonged, for the most part, also to one political party and one religious denomination. The philanthropists, lawyers and statesmen who busied themselves in the course of the eighteenth century with such matters as prisons and pauperism, highways and bridges, all alike proposed, in their various schemes of reform, to extend the powers of the County Justices, either as direct administrators of their own institutions and services, or as local legislators dictating a policy to subordinate authorities. This unhesitating acceptance of the landed gentry as an autonomous County oligarchy is to be seen reflected in parliamentary procedure as well as in legislation. So far as the internal local administration of the rural districts was concerned the House of Commons felt itself to be scarcely more than a legislative 'clearing house' of the several Courts of Quarter Sessions. The Knights of the Shire who sat at Westminster habitually regarded themselves as the spokesmen of these Courts, from which they received instructions as to Bills to be promoted, supported, amended or opposed. To give an instance among many: when Whitbread brought in his comprehensive Poor Law Bill in 1807 it was taken for granted that it would be circulated to the Justices. Rose, latterly Pitt's ablest subordinate, thought that 'it might go to Quarter Sessions in its present shape'. Another Tory member objected that 'the opinion of the Justices could not be collected at the next Quarter Sessions' on so extensive a Bill, and urged that it should 'be divided into parts for their consideration', a course which Whitbread thought it prudent to adopt.[1] The student will now realise what we meant by the assertion that, in spite of the apparently centralized legal constitution of English Local Government, and of the complete dependence in law of the Commission of the Peace on the will of the monarch and his ministers, at no period did the landed gentry enjoy so large a measure of local autonomy and irresponsible power as between the accession of the House of Hanover and the close of the Napoleonic wars. It was this 'local self-government' of each County by a Commission of the Peace made up of voluntarily serving territorial magnates and landed gentry, that seemed, to Rudolf von Gneist, the greatest foreign student of English Local Government, the most unique, distinctive and admirable feature of the British constitution.

Local Customs and the Common Law as the Foundation of Local Institutions

We pass now from the principles embodied in the structure and function of the old-established local institutions of the eighteenth century to the subsoil of local customs and the Common Law[2] in which these institutions were deeply rooted.

[1] *The Parish and the County*, pp. 554–5.

[2] F. W. Maitland thus defines Common Law: '. . . This term common law, which we have been using, needs some explanation. I think that it comes into use in or shortly after

We can imagine no more unpleasant nightmare for the meticulous-minded solicitor of today, acting as clerk to a Town or County Council, or a Rural or Urban District Council, than to find himself suddenly in the eighteenth century, and called upon to act as steward of the Manor, clerk of the Vestry, chamberlain to some Municipal Corporation or Clerk of the Peace to Quarter Sessions. Listening with bewilderment to what was taking place around him, his first instinct would be to call for the Act of Parliament determining the constitution, the procedure and the activities of the body that he was called upon to advise and serve. To the little group of tenants who appeared before him as steward of the Manor in the guise of manorial officers or members of the Leet Jury, the question would have been meaningless: they would have told him that their right to declare the customs of the Manor, to make presentments and to give verdicts, as well as their obligation to serve, came down from 'time out of mind', and that there were no Acts of Parliament which affected them. The little knot of Parish Officers and principal inhabitants, who formed the Vestry to which he acted as clerk, would have been puzzled at his question. The chairman, who was also the incumbent of the Parish and probably himself a Justice of the Peace, would assert that the Parish

the reign of Edward the First. The word "common" of course is not opposed to "uncommon": rather it means "general", and the contrast to common law is special law. Common law is in the first place unenacted law; thus it is distinguished from statutes and ordinances. In the second place, it is common to the whole land; thus it is distinguished from local customs. In the third place, it is the law of the temporal courts; thus it is distinguished from ecclesiastical law.'

Officers took their orders from the Justices; and that with regard to these orders he had better look up the noted work of the Rev. Richard Burn, a contemporary clerical Justice; but that he doubted whether there would be anything in it about the constitution of the Vestry. If this clerical Justice happened also to be a man of learning he might proceed to tell the ignorant clerk that neither the King by charter, nor the High Court of Parliament by statute, had ever endowed the Parish with a precise constitution, or even with any constitution at all. With respect to some of the most important of its features—such, for instance, as its area and boundaries,[1] the number and method of appointment of its most characteristic officers, and their powers of taxation—the Parish had no better warrant than ancient tradition, handed down from generation to generation, seldom embodied in any document, and admittedly differing from place to place according to local usage, of which no one outside the locality concerned had any exact knowledge. A modern solicitor would find himself even more distressed by the constitution of a Municipal Corporation

[1] 'The settling parochial rights or the bounds of parishes', says Archbishop Stillingfleet, 'depends upon an ancient and immemorial custom. For they were not limited by any Act of Parliament, nor set forth by special commissioners, but as the circumstances of times and places and persons did happen to make them greater or lesser' (*Ecclesiastical Cases Relative to Duties and Rights of Parochial Clergy, &c.*, by Edward Stillingfleet, 1698, Part I, p. 348; *The Parish and the County*, p. 9). Thus, the Vestries of Tooting and Streatham, in 1808, in connexion with 'beating the bounds' of their respective parishes, formally agreed by resolutions to exchange certain strips of land and groups of houses, with apparently no thought that this matter concerned anyone but themselves (*The Parish and the County*, 1907, p. 53).

of the eighteenth century. As Chamberlain to the City of London, for instance, he would have been told that the Corporation consisted of an agglomeration of distinct Courts,[1] originating at different periods and for different purposes, deriving their authority indifferently from immemorial prescription and royal charter. Rigid constitution there was none, seeing that the Corporation claimed and exercised the right of altering its own constitution without the interference of Parliament. The Clerk of the Peace of today might hope to find himself more at home attending a Court of Quarter Sessions in the eighteenth century. Of Acts of Parliament, indeed there was no lack, dealing with the poor, the vagrants, the highways and so on. But he would be disheartened to discover that there was no statute establishing or even describing his own office; that his fees were regulated only by local custom, and it was long uncertain whether or not the Justices of the Peace could lawfully dispute his charges. Moreover, the whole procedure of presentment by Juries of the defective highways and bridges left it uncertain what works could be ordered by the

[1] In our chapter on 'The Municipal Corporation' we show that a Municipal Corporation, like the Manor and unlike the Parish and the County, was, in fact, not primarily a territorial expression. 'It was a bundle of jurisdictions relating to persons, and only incidentally to the place in which those persons happened to be. But beyond this simple form, every additional jurisdiction, it is scarcely too much to say, involved, for its operation, a separate and different geographical area. There was one at least of the Municipal Franchises that had no geographical limits whatever, though it is precisely the one which today we associate most directly with definite boundaries, namely, the right to return Burgesses to sit in Parliament.'

Justices, and whether they could assess the inhabitants for the widening of a road or the making of a new bridge.[1] And when the Clerk of the Peace followed the Justices into the parlour of the tavern where, over their walnuts and wine, they issued general instructions to keep and cause to be kept the King's peace, he would be startled to find that the Justices considered themselves (as Ritson complained in 1791) 'a sort of legislative body', having power to determine the behaviour of their fellow-citizens; to forbid fairs, wakes, revels and any meetings they objected to; to shut up public houses, and even to give to the principal inhabitants of the townships the option of closing any public houses which they or a majority of them might consider to be ill-conducted or unnecessary.[2] Or the Justices might require every Petty Constable within the County to report to them 'what number of men and women servants each inhabitant within his constabulary hath, and what quality and what wages every master gives to every particular servant'; in order that the Justices might settle what wages should be paid in future. The

[1] In 1710, relates a lively writer in the *Gentleman's Magazine*, 'I remember a gentleman went to the Quarter Sessions holden at Easter in a Northern County, to oppose' certain expenditure on a bridge, 'for which £130, as an introductory sum, had been paid by the Petty Constables to the Chief. The lawyer he retained addressing himself to the Court, said, Gentlemen, you must maintain the ancient bridges, but have no authority to build new ones where there never were any, without an Act of Parliament. Then moved for a discharge of the order granted before, and for repayment of the money, which were agreed to without objection, every Petty Constable soon after receiving his respective share.' (*The Story of the King's Highway*, by S. and B. Webb, 1913, pp. 95–96.)

[2] *The Parish and the County*, p. 536.

Justices would even take upon themselves to alter Local Government areas, to dictate the basis of assessment to the local rates and even to divide the County into two or more entirely autonomous districts, with separate finances, separate County properties and separate rates; whilst, as Cobbett indignantly pointed out in 1822, enactments vitally affecting the right of the destitute person to poor relief could be made in the name of the Hampshire Court of Quarter Sessions by 'two squires' and 'five parsons' from behind the closed doors of the 'Grand Jury Room'.[1] Even the Justices themselves would occasionally complain of the informality and legislative assumptions of their so-called 'deliberative assemblies'. 'I observed a paragraph and advertisement', deprecatingly writes an eminent Suffolk magistrate in 1793, who objected to the device of a legally prescribed non-competitive wage, 'in your paper of yesterday, reporting a resolution passed at the Quarter Sessions held at Bury. I assuredly did not concur in it; but, as far as I understood it to be before the company as a matter of conversation (for I did not contemplate it as a question before the Sessions), I opposed it, and the resolve must have passed in my absence.'[2] The Clerk of the Peace, in fact, was as powerless to control the Justices as the Justices were to control him. All the authority of the Justices was in its nature judicial; it was concerned with the enforcement of the obligations of individuals or of corporations, or of

[1] Cobbett's *Political Register*, 21 September 1822; *The Parish and the County*, p. 551. See the 'Berkshire Bread Act' or 'Speenhamland Act of Parliament' (ibid. pp. 544–50).

[2] Capel Lofft to the editor of the *Bury Post*, 15 October 1795; *The Parish and the County*, p. 551.

pseudo-corporate bodies, under the law of the land. Once the Justices abandoned judicial procedure and retired from the 'Open Court' into their private room, for mingled deliberation and conviviality, it became exceedingly doubtful whether all their proceedings were not extra-legal in character, and without formal authority.

The dependence of local administration on local customs and the Common Law had curiously conflicting results. It meant that from one end of England to the other, each of the Local Authorities enjoyed, in practice, an almost unchecked autonomy, unless and until any of its actions or decisions happened to be brought into a Court of Law. The autonomy of the Parish was checked by the subordination of its officers to the local Justices of the Peace, but the autonomy of the Manor, of the Manorial Borough and of the Municipal Corporation could only be questioned by suit in the Courts at Westminster, a very expensive and uncertain method of redress. As for the Justices of the Peace, they were judges to enforce their own decisions, and any individual Justices or local bench of Justices could do practically anything they liked so long as they had Quarter Sessions on their side. The Court of Quarter Sessions itself was subject to no formal appellate jurisdiction, and equally to no external audit or systematic scrutiny of its proceedings, the legality of which could be challenged only by action in the Courts of King's Bench, Common Pleas or Exchequer. Notwithstanding the expense and trouble of such an action, it was through the public spirit or obstinacy of aggrieved or recalcitrant individuals that, once or twice, in every generation, led to authoritative judicial decisions, which determined, until the next time that the issue was tried, what were the qualifications and obligations, the powers and the duties, of the several officers of the Parish and County; within what limits the Manorial Court could, by creating new nuisances, active or passive, prescribe the conduct of the local residents or mulct them in fines; in what sense the frequently conflicting charters of a Manorial Borough or a Municipal Corporation were to be understood, and how far their decaying authority could be stretched to meet new circumstances; what the Courts of Sewers could command in the way of assessments to make new sewers, and how the Sewers Juries were to be summoned; and how the obligation of the Parish to keep up its highways and those of the County to maintain its bridges could be construed to include the new methods of roadmaking, and the upkeep of bridges of the very existence of which the County had had no official cognizance. It must be remembered that, in every such action, the Courts of Law decided, in terms, no more than the liability of a particular defendant in a particular issue. There was no general promulgation, and not even any official report of the decisions. The enterprise of publishers and unofficial law-reporters provided an ever-growing number of volumes of 'Reports of Cases', which were hard to read and still harder to construe. The decisions were not always consistent with each other; and it remained in all cases uncertain in what sense future judges would apply them to the differing circumstances of future actions. What was supposed to be the law might at any moment be completely changed

—as we have shown to have happened, for instance, with regard to the legality of Select Vestries, and with regard to the liability of the County to maintain privately constructed bridges—if a new case was brought before a different judge, presented with additional knowledge of former precedents and existing facts, and argued by more learned or more ingenious counsel. The popular manuals of Local Government law from 'Burn' to 'Stone' strove in vain to condense this voluminous mass of 'case law' into a systematic code to be relied upon as legally authoritative and at the same time understandable by the country gentleman or sorely perplexed Overseer.

But though, in the absence of general statutes prescribing the constitution and powers of the various Local Authorities, there existed a local autonomy amounting almost to anarchy, there was grave difficulty in enforcing, against any recalcitrant offender, any judgment or decision whatsoever. The Court of the Manor could 'amerce' but not imprison; and it was popularly supposed that no amercement could exceed forty shillings. Wealthy sinners preferred to pay the fine and continue the offence. The Justices of the Peace might, in practice, be as autocratic as they chose; but they were sometimes checked by Lords of Manors who threatened to take a prohibition of fairs or markets into the Courts at Westminster, as an infringement of their property rights. Moreover, against the judgments of a 'Single' or a 'Double' Justice, there was an appeal to Quarter Sessions; and always the possibility of the case being carried to Westminster on a point of law. What was more serious was that serious breaches of the law could only be dealt with by the dilatory and expensive process of indictment, just as civil actions for debts or damages involved, in the usual absence of any petty debt-court in the locality itself, a costly and long-delayed action in the King's Courts. Thus, the great mass of common people could be, in practice, autocratically governed, and even harried and oppressed by arbitrary taxation; whilst the wealthy person could, by threatening to take the case to Westminster, or fight the matter at the Assizes, go far to reduce authority to a nullity. It was, more than anything else, this uncertainty of the law and of the powers of the various Local Government Courts and officers, coupled with the growing need for summary jurisdiction in dealing with offenders or recalcitrants, that gradually led to the establishment of new Statutory Authorities for Special Purposes, the steady increase in the kinds of cases which the magistrates could deal with summarily, and (in the early part of the nineteenth century) the enactment of general statutes seeking to systematize, and to codify for universal application, the laws relating to the various functions of Local Government. To the dismay and regret of those who, like Toulmin Smith,[1] upheld the ancient autonomy of the Parish and the Manor, and the supremacy of immemorial local customs and the Common Law, the whole field of Local Government came gradually to be dominated

[1] In a remarkable series of volumes between 1848 and 1870, the erudite and conservative-minded J. Toulmin Smith idealises under the term 'Local Self-Government' the autonomy arising out of the Common Law of England and local customs interpreted by Juries of inhabitants.

by Acts of Parliament. The active control of the structure and function of local governing bodies by the National Legislature was one of the new principles gradually evolved in the course of the eighteenth century.

Chapter Two

THE EMERGENCE OF THE NEW PRINCIPLES

WE have now to consider what were the new ideas of social organization, or the new principles of government, by which the old-established local institutions of the Manor and the Borough, the Parish and the County were gradually transformed. These new principles of government were not introduced deliberately, suddenly or universally: they gradually emerged in different decades in different places, with varying degrees of awareness on the part of their promoters and opponents. It is, in fact, only 'by being wise after the event' that we can isolate each principle, and trace its evolution as a process of continual action and reaction between the new physical and mental environment, on the one hand, and the waxing and waning activities of the various organs of Local Government on the other. 'It is not only from the point of view of logical distinctions', declares Professor Vinagradoff, 'that analogies and contrasts in law have to be considered. It is clear that there is a background of social conditions which account to a great extent for the stages of the doctrinal evolution.'[1]

To enable this revolution in the principles of Local Government to be understood, we open this chapter

[1] *Essays in Legal History*, edited by Professor Paul Vinagradoff, 1913, p. 7.

with a brief survey of the changes that were occurring, in the course of the eighteenth and the first quarter of the nineteenth century, in the life and labour of the English people. We proceed to discuss some of the novel concepts and new methods of thought that partly arose from, and partly gave birth to the changes in the material environment. But our main task in this concluding chapter will be to disentangle and to analyse the distinctive principles resulting from the new physical and mental circumstances in which the various local institutions had to operate: circumstances effecting so momentous a transformation in both parish and county administration, and stimulating the establishment of so many new Statutory Authorities, as eventually to render almost inevitable the revolutionary reconstructions of the Municipal Corporations Act and the Poor Law Amendment Act.

The main forces transforming the environment of English local institutions between the Revolution and the Municipal Corporations Act were, first, the Industrial Revolution (in its largest sense, including agriculture and commerce) doubling the numbers, altering the geographical distribution and transforming the status and the circumstances of the English people; and, secondly, the new conceptions of political liberty and personal freedom, arising, possibly, in connexion with religious nonconformity, subsequently manifested in and advertised by the American and French Revolutions, and incorporated in Great Britain in the administrative and legislative projects of the Utilitarian school of social philosophy.

The Industrial Revolution in Relation to Local Institutions

We are not here concerned with the two outstanding and dramatic results of the Industrial Revolution: on the one hand, the enormous increase in wealth and power of the British Empire through its dominance of the world markets; and, on the other, the transformation of the great bulk of the inhabitants of England from independent producers, owning the instruments and the product of their labour, into a vast wage-earning proletariate, in large part subsisting always on the brink of destitution and chronic pauperism. The student who concentrates on one or other of these aspects may regard this period either as the most glorious or the most infamous in English history. The investigator into the contemporary developments of English local institutions finds the resulting transformations alike more complicated and less easy to value one against the other.

The Massing of Men

The most obvious of the changes made by the Industrial Revolution in the circumstances of the Parish and the County, the Manor and the Borough, was the vast increase in population, and the new massing of men, women and children in particular areas, a process steadily intensified from the close of the eighteenth century onward. When William of Orange landed at Tor Bay his future English subjects numbered fewer than six millions; and these, apart from the exceptional aggregation of the Metropolis, were scattered, more or less evenly, throughout all the

Counties of England, from Cornwall to Berwick, from Harwich to Holyhead. They lived, for the most part, in tiny hamlets and small villages, surrounded by wastes and common fields, with here and there a market town or cathedral city, enclosing within its ancient boundaries a hundred or two, or, at most, a thousand old-established households of traders and master craftsmen. Omitting for the moment the anomalous City of London, with its outlying villages, and the ancient cities of Bristol and Norwich, which counted each thirty thousand inhabitants, there were, in 1689, no towns of even twenty thousand—a figure not reached at that date by either York or Exeter—whilst only half-a-dozen others exceeded five thousand. The unique aggregation in the Metropolitan area alone could boast of half a million people. A hundred years afterwards the total population had reached nine millions, and when England emerged triumphant from the Napoleonic wars it had increased to nearly twelve millions, having doubled its population within a century and a quarter. But even more important than the growth in total numbers was the ever-increasing concentration of these new masses in densely crowded industrial centres. By 1835 the bulk of the English people were no longer country folk engaged in agriculture and domestic handicrafts; an actual majority of them had become denizens of the mean streets springing up in irregular agglomerations, for the most part outside the jurisdiction of any Municipal Corporation. Over large parts of Middlesex, Surrey, Lancashire, and the West Riding of Yorkshire, in Durham and Nottinghamshire, in Birmingham and the Midlands, the Juries of the

Lord's Court or the Church-wardens and Overseers and principal inhabitants in Vestry assembled, found themselves dealing, not with a little group of neighbours centring round church and manor-house, but with uncounted hordes of unknown men, women and children, crowded together in hastily built tenements; with the ancient King's highway, which had become encumbered with wagons and travelling beasts, transformed into streets lined with warehouses, with here and there a factory, forge or mine, each employing hundreds, and even thousands of 'hands', and contaminating the ground, the streams and the air with its output of filthy refuse—a neighbourhood from which the country gentleman and the incumbent, who alone were Justices of the Peace, had usually withdrawn to more agreeable places of residence. Exactly where the local institutions were of the weakest type, the population became the greatest. Some of the old Municipal Corporations, with their own magistrates and corporate officers, often with their own representatives in the House of Commons, had shrunk into rural hamlets, whilst elsewhere the Manorial and Parish Officers often found themselves the only Local Authorities in densely peopled and rapidly increasing mining or manufacturing areas.

The Devastating Torrent of Public Nuisances

Without citing illustrative cases, as described by contemporaries, it is not easy to make the student understand the extent and the disastrous characters of the changes in the physical environment of the common people wrought by the Industrial Revolution, notably in the latter part of the period under review. The successful warehousemen or millowners in and around Manchester, for instance, who were between 1763 and 1832 growing rich beyond the dreams of avarice, failed entirely to realize the inroads which their profit-making enterprise was making upon the common conditions of healthy existence. Even as late as 1795 Manchester, as pictured in Aikin's classic work,[1] lay in the midst of smiling meadows and well-growing plantations, interspersed with ponds stocked with perch and pike, and clear streams yielding abundantly both of trout and salmon. But in the town itself, as we have indicated, the worst nuisances were already rife. In the last decade of the eighteenth century, it could be said by a medical man that, 'in some parts of the town, cellars are so damp as to be unfit for habitation'; that there is one street in which 'is a range of cellars let out to lodgers which threaten to become a nursery of diseases'; that 'near the extremities of the town . . . the lodging-houses . . . produce many fevers . . . by want of cleanliness and air.'[2] Thirty years later, all these kinds of nuisances were found in undiminished intensity with the important difference that, instead of one such street or group of underground dwellings or lodging-houses there were, in 1830, literally thousands in the same awful state. This meant that the wretched inhabitants of these cellars and tenement houses had become, not only more densely crowded together, but

[1] *A Description of the Country from Thirty to Forty Miles round Manchester*, by Dr. John Aikin, 1795.

[2] Dr. Ferrier's Report to a Committee, quoted in *A Description of the Country . . . round Manchester*, by J. Aikin, 1795, p. 193.

also increasingly hemmed in, so that their whole lives were passed in the slums. The growth of Manchester, together with the corresponding transformation of Salford, Stockport, Stalybridge, Hyde, Ashton, and other townships, had, for miles in every direction, defiled the atmosphere, polluted the streams and destroyed the vegetation. Whilst the Manchester Police Commissioners had been widening one or two main thoroughfares for their own lorries and carriages; or imperfectly paving, lighting, cleansing and watching the principal streets in which their own mansions and warehouses were situated, unregulated private enterprise had been covering the green fields with mile upon mile of squalid 'back to back' cottages, crammed close together in narrow courts and blind alleys; with underground cellars occupied indifferently by human beings, animals and stores of cinders and filth; with dunghills, middens and open cesspools in which every conceivable refuse lay putrefying. The enormous multiplication of steam-engines, and the growth of every kind of industry had, in spite of the half-hearted admonitions of the Authorities, both deepened and broadened the pall of black smoke, which ever overhung the houses, and from which every fall of rain brought down showers of soot. Inside the town the continued increase of population had augmented every evil. The few private slaughter-houses, which had in old days supplemented the shambles of the market-place, had grown to nearly fourscore, stowed away in back yards, closed courts or even underground cellars, which they infected with putrefying blood, offal and filth. When in 1832 the outbreak of cholera led to 'an inspection of the town, conducted under the orders of a well-organized Board of Health', they were 'disclosed in the quarters of the poor . . . scenes of filth and crowding and dilapidation', which could, we think, hardly have been paralleled in character, and certainly not in extent, in any city, at any previous period whatsoever. Out of no more than 687 streets inspected, there were 248 wholly unpaved, '53 paved partially, 112 ill-ventilated (closed-in courts, &c.), 352 which have heaps of refuse and stagnant pools at the doors'; whilst, out of 6,951 houses inspected, 2,221, or nearly a third, were found to be destitute of any kind of sanitary accommodation whatsoever. Throughout one whole quarter of the town, reports the Board of Health, 'the privies are in a most disgraceful state, inaccessible from filth, and too few for the accommodation of the number of people, the average number being two to 250 people. The upper rooms are, with a few exceptions, very dirty, and the cellars much worse; all damp and some occasionally overflowed. The cellars consist of two rooms on a floor, each nine to ten feet square, some inhabited by ten persons, others by more; in many the people have no beds and keep each other warm by close stowage, on shavings, straw, &c. A change of linen or clothes is an exception to the general practice. Many of the back rooms where they sleep have no other means of ventilation than from the front rooms.'[1] The deplorable result of free 'and

[1] MS. Minutes, Local Board of Health, Manchester, 21 December 1832. (Report of Special Sub-committee on 'Little Ireland' district.) Part of this is printed in the *General Report on the Sanitary Condition of the Labouring Population of Great Britain*, 1842, p. 39.

unregulated private enterprise' in the development of building estates was, indeed, apparent in every growing town, not excluding the Metropolis itself. 'The principle of speculation', reports a Marylebone resident in 1814, 'is to take large tracts of ground by the acre, and to crowd as many streets and lanes into it as they can, in order to create so many feet lineal [of frontage] to underlet for building; and the fruit of the speculation is the sale of the increased ground rents. These houses are therefore of the meanest sort; are built of the worst and slightest materials, and but for their dependence on each other for support, would, many of them, not stand the term of their leases. . . . A very few years will exhibit cracked walls, sagged floors, bulged front, crooked roofs, leaky gutters, inadequate drains and other ills of an originally bad construction.'[1] An observer of 1768 reports that, 'in one morning's walk which we took along the Strand last week, we counted no less than seventy odd houses made up of nothing but laths and plaster—a frightful number this in a street the most frequented of the whole town; and no wonder that so many fires are continually alarming the Metropolis while such edifices as those are suffered to stand in various parts of it.'[2] But it was not only the jerry builder who was at work. Between 1806 and 1816 the Paving Committee of the Joint Vestries of St. Margaret and St. John, Westminster, carried on a prolonged wrangle with the new joint stock gas and water companies, whom they denounced for 'so

[1] *Some Account of the Proposed Improvements of the Western Part of London*, 1814, pp. xxv, xxviii.

[2] *The Occasionalist*, No. XIV, 1769.

frequently disturbing the pavement', and thereby heedlessly increasing by their works and omissions the dangerous obstruction of the streets. The 'dilapidation of the pavements', which had, in 1816, attracted the attention of the House of Commons, was ascribed by the Select Committee to 'the frequency with which the numerous water and gas companies, as well as the Commissioners of Sewers, disturb the pavements, to the great inconvenience of the public, and to the severe loss and expense of the districts which they pervade.'[1] 'All the competition or rivalry which they produced', declared in 1819 a spokesman of the Vestries in the House of Commons, 'was the rivalry of who should pull the pavement most violently to pieces.'[2] 'It is highly desirable', concluded a leading Manchester citizen in 1834, 'that the inhabitants . . . should have the ownership of works' for gas and water, on account of the 'breaking up of the streets''.[3]

To any Englishman of the present day, who found himself suddenly transported to the London or Birmingham, the Liverpool or Sheffield of a century ago, the most striking feature would probably be the 'general nastiness' of the ground he trod upon, defiled by an almost incredible accumulation of every kind of filth. He might next notice the noisome and all-pervading stench, which was so customary and continuous as to be scarcely ever commented upon. A specially disgusting instance is given by an anonymous writer

[1] *Report of the Select Committee on the Present State of the Pavement of the Metropolis*, 1816, p. 3.

[2] *Hansard*, 17 May 1819.

[3] Speech of Thomas Hopkins, *Manchester Times*, 25 January 1834.

early in the eighteenth century. The Parish Authorities, he writes, 'dig in the churchyards or other annexed burial-places large holes or pits in which they put many of the bodies of those whose friends are not able to pay for better graves; and then those pits or holes (called the Poor's Holes) once opened are not covered till filled with such dead bodies. Thus it is in St. Martin's, St. James's, St. Giles in the Fields and other places. . . . How noisome the stench is that arises from these holes so stow'd with dead bodies, especially in sultry seasons and after rain one may appeal to all who approach them.'[1] A hundred years later, there was, at Bristol, in 1822, 'generally two or three times a week, a most sickening and offensive vapour', supposed, we are told, to arise from the gas works or salt refinery, 'which hangs over the whole city for about two hours, whose noxious effluvia is capable of awakening the soundest sleeper, and interrupting the respiration of all who have not very strong lungs.'[2] Another way in which the air was habitually polluted by poisonous stench was the result of the much-valued practice of keeping pigs in back yards, front areas, cellars and even inside rooms. This prevailed to an incredible extent in every town, not excluding the Metropolis itself. At Rochester in 1673, the Municipal Corporation, whilst objecting to pigs roaming at large, expressly sanctioned their being kept in the citizens' houses.[3] In 1768 Sir John Fielding declared that this particular 'evil . . . is

[1] *Some Customs considered, whether prejudicial to the Health of this City* (n.d. ? 1721), pp. 7, 10.

[2] *Bristol Journal*, 10 August 1822.

[3] *An Authentic Copy of the Charter and By-laws of the City of Rochester*, 1809, p. 35.

increased to an enormous degree; and a number of sows for breeding, and other hogs are kept in cellars and other confined places in the City and Liberty of Westminster, which are very offensive and unwholesome.'[1] In the notorious district of Kensington, known as 'the Potteries', nearly every family kept pigs, which 'usually outnumbered the people three to one, and had their styes mixed up with the dwelling houses".[2] The almost universal pollution of the water supply in every aggregation of people, which inevitably resulted from the dirt and filth of the thoroughfares, and the absence of any means of disposing of excreta, was, as we now realize, a constant cause of disease. The dense swarms of pallid, undersized and wretchedly clothed wage-earners, who constituted all but a tiny minority of the population, might have been noticed, by a twentieth century observer, to be perpetually suffering from ill-health, and to be, in fact, practically all either sickening for or recovering from attacks of what we should now term either enteric or typhus. Whilst the number of births everywhere increased by leaps and bounds—coincidently with the common abandonment of the practice of the 'living in' of farm labourers and town apprentices and journeymen—the death rate was, at all ages, enormous. There are, in fact, indications that, during the eighteenth as doubtless during the fourteenth century, in the worst areas in the slums of the great towns—continually recruited by immigration from the rural

[1] *Extracts*, &c., by Sir John Fielding, pp. 100–3.

[2] *The Observance of the Sanitary Laws Divinely Appointed*, by the Rev. Charles Richson, with notes by Dr. John Sutherland, 1854, p. 12.

districts—the mortality actually exceeded the births.[1]

The Growth of Pauperism

The catastrophic transformation in the physical environment of large sections of the inhabitants of England, in the homes they lived in, in the ground they trod, in the water they drank and in the air they breathed, was accompanied by an equally drastic change in the circumstances, the amount and the security of their livelihood. We do not need to repeat the eloquent description by Mr. and Mrs. Hammond of the effect, on the one hand, of the enclosures on the agricultural worker, and on the other, of the novel capitalist industry on the new class of wage-operatives. 'How much', they exclaim, 'the working classes lost in happiness, in physical energy, in moral power, in the inherited stamina of mind and body, during the years when these overwhelming forces were pressing them down, it is impossible to estimate.'[2] What seemed more relevant to the Church-wardens and Overseers, and to the little meeting of principal inhabitants in Vestry assembled, as well as to the County Justices, was the continuous growth of pauperism, which dates, in many parts of England, from the very beginning of the eighteenth century. Instead of merely having to succour by doles a few dozen or a few score of aged or sick neighbours, individually known and complacently

[1] We do not suggest that sanitary conditions may not have been quite as bad in the crowded towns of the fifteenth century as in those of the eighteenth century. But prior to the eighteenth century the town population was small.

[2] *The Town Labourer*, by J. L. and Barbara Hammond, 1917, p. 141. See also *The Village Labourer*, 1912, and *The Skilled Labourer*, 1919, by the same authors.

tolerated in their indigence, the Church-wardens and Overseers of Parish after Parish found themselves confronted with the administrative difficulties attendant on maintaining hundreds and sometimes even thousands, of men, women and children, often immigrants from other Parishes, whose circumstances were unknown to the Officers, and whose requirements seemed to threaten a serious inroad on the incomes of the minority of solvent ratepayers. We have described elsewhere in writing on the Incorporated Guardians of the Poor how this problem led to the establishment of new Local Authorities, which erected workhouses and experimented, with uniform but constantly repeated ill-success, in 'setting the poor to work' to produce their own maintenance. In our description of the activities of the Justices of the Peace, in legislating for the County, we have seen them reverting to the simpler device of Outdoor Relief, which they elaborated by 'the Allowance System', into a comprehensive scheme of making up eveybody's earnings to a prescribed minimum, varying with the price of bread. The peace of 1815 brought with it social conditions even worse than those of the couple of decades of war. 'From the beginning of 1816, England was visited by an unexampled stagnation of trade. The poor', said Brand in the House of Commons on 28 March 1816, 'in many cases have abandoned their own residences. Whole Parishes have been deserted, and the crowd of paupers increasing in numbers as they go from Parish to Parish, spread wider and wider this awful desolation.'[1]

[1] *Hansard*, vol. xxxiii, p. 671; *The Life of Francis Place, 1711–1854*, by Graham Wallas, 1898, p. 114.

All this new destitution, complicated by the Law of Settlement and the Allowance System, confronted the unpaid Parish Officers with intricate administrative and financial problems which they were wholly unable to solve. At the beginning of the eighteenth century the total Poor Rate levied throughout England scarcely reached one million pounds. During the ensuing three-quarters of a century it rose slowly to a million and three-quarters. Between 1776 and 1785 it suddenly bounded up by 25 per cent. At the beginning of the nineteenth century it had risen to over four million pounds, by 1813 to nearly seven million, and by 1818 to nearly eight millions. Meanwhile the rates levied by the new Improvement Commissioners, who were feebly grappling with the outburst of public nuisances, together with the rising County Rate for bridges and prisons, added substantially to the local burden. Moreover, the task of assessing and collecting the rates had been completely altered from the informal agreement among a group of neighbours, as to the contributions in respect of their old-established homes or holdings, into a series of elaborate calculations without the data by which alone such assessments could be made on any equitable basis. The bewildered Church-wardens and Overseers were confronted, not only with streets on streets of dwellings of every sort and description, but also with the multitudes of newly erected forges and factories, blast-furnaces and warehouses, not to mention the newly opened collieries and canals. How was it possible for the Parish Officers to estimate the rental value of premises which had never been in the market, and the size of which, measured in three dimensions, still more the cost, was wholly beyond the capacity of their imaginations? The mere collection of the greatly swollen rates from thousands of shifting occupiers, to say nothing of the control of an expenditure which had risen to unexampled sums, involved, in itself, a transformation of the machinery of Local Government.

The Increase in Crime

To the noblemen and gentlemen to whom, as Justices, was committed the keeping of the King's peace, there was a consequence even more sinister than the rise in the Poor Rate. The transformation of the bulk of the English nation from a settled population of yeomen cultivators, peasant copyholders, domestic handicraftsmen and 'small masters', owning the instruments and the product of their labour, and accepting without question the existing order of society, into a migratory swarm of propertyless wage-earners, crowded together in the labyrinths of houses characteristic of the Metropolis, the great ports and the new urban centres, inevitably meant an enormous increase of disorder, licentiousness and crime. There is, we think, reason to agree with contemporary writers, that the overgrown and unorganized conglomeration of houses of the Metropolitan area was, from the beginning to the end of the eighteenth century, pre-eminent in criminality. We despair of conveying any adequate picture of the lawless violence, the barbarous licentiousness, and the almost unlimited opportunities for pilfering and robbery offered by the unpoliced London streets of that century. Down to 1697 the whole districts of Whitefriars and the Savoy were, by immemorial custom, sanctuaries, into the precincts of which no officer of justice ventured; and though these privileges were taken away by statute in that year, the crowded streets and alleys of 'the Mint', in Southwark, maintained a similar immunity until 1723. But even without legal privileges, the very size of the Metropolis, with its bewildering mass of narrow thoroughfares, served as one vast sanctuary, from which thieves could sally out in practical safety. 'Whoever, indeed, considers', said Henry Fielding, 'the cities of London and Westminster, with the late vast addition of their suburbs, the great irregularity of their buildings, the immense number of lanes, alleys, courts and bye-places, must think that, had they been intended for the very purpose of concealment, they could scarce have been better contrived. Upon such a view, the whole appears as a vast wood or forest, in which a thief may harbour with as great security as wild beasts do in the deserts of Africa or Arabia; for by wandering from one part to another and often shifting his quarters, he may almost avoid the possibility of being discovered.' Innumerable references occur, from 1700 onward, to 'the frequency of street robberies of late years'.[1] 'London', writes Shenstone in 1743, 'is really dangerous at this time; the pickpockets, formerly content with mere filching, make no scruple to knock people down with bludgeons in Fleet Street and the Strand, and that at no later hour than eight o'clock at night; but in the Piazzas, Covent Garden, they come in large bodies armed with *couteaus* and attack whole

[1] *London Journal*, 19 March 1726.

parties, so that the danger of coming out of the play-houses is of some weight in the opposite scale when I am disposed to go to them oftener than I should.'[1] Shenstone's account is borne out by official documents. 'Divers confederacies of great numbers of evil-disposed persons', declared the Common Council of the City of London in 1744, 'armed with bludgeons, pistols, cutlasses and other dangerous weapons, infest not only the private lanes and passages but likewise the public streets and places of usual concourse, and commit most daring outrages upon the persons of your Majesty's good subjects whose affairs oblige them to pass through the streets, by robbing and wounding them; and these acts are frequently perpetrated at such times as were heretofore deemed hours of security.'[2] 'One is forced to travel', wrote Horace Walpole in 1752, 'even at noon, as if one were going to battle.' So great was the 'increase of robberies within these few years,' wrote Fielding in 1753, 'that the streets of this town, and the roads leading to it, will shortly be impassable without the utmost hazard; nor are we threatened with seeing less dangerous gangs of rogues among us than those which the Italians call the Banditti'.[3] From London these gangs of robbers, and individual pilferers, radiated into the country on all sides. We have the high authority of Sir John Fielding for the statement that 'There are more highway robberies

[1] Letter by Shenstone in 1743 (*Works*, 3rd edition, vol. iii, p. 73).

[2] MS. Minutes, Court of Aldermen, City of London, 1774; given in *Eighteenth Century*, by J. Andrews, p. 230.

[3] *An Enquiry into the Causes of the late Increase of Robbers, &c.*, by H. Fielding, 1751.

committed . . . within twenty miles of London than . . . in the whole kingdom besides.'[1] 'The robberies', says a newspaper of 1754, 'are chiefly in and about London; and even when they happen in the country, they are generally committed by rogues, who make excursions out of London at fairs, horse races and other public meetings; which clearly and evidently points out the true cause of them to be the overgrown size of London, affording infinite receptacles to sharpers, thieves and villains of all kinds. In the villages adjacent to the Metropolis, scarce any one resident therein, be his condition ever so low, can call anything his own.' Right down to the end of the eighteenth century the neighbourhood of the great Metropolis continued to present the same scene of disorder and rapine. 'The fields near London', wrote Middleton in 1798, 'are never free from men strolling about, in pilfering pursuits by day, and committing greater crimes by night.'[2] 'No one', said Colquhoun in 1800, 'could be approaching the Capital in any direction after dark, without risk of being assaulted and robbed, and perhaps wounded or murdered. We cannot lay down to rest in our habitations without the dread of a burglary being committed, our property invaded, and our lives

[1] *A Plan for Preventing Robberies within 20 miles of London*, by Sir John Fielding, 1755, p. 7; see also his *Extracts from such of the Penal Laws as particularly relate to the Peace and Good Order of the Metropolis*, 1768. 'Housebreaking in London', records the *Annual Register* for 1770, 'was never known to be so frequent; seldom a night passing but some house or other was entered and robbed' (p. 78).

[2] *General View of the Agriculture of Middlesex* by John Middleton, 1798, p. 460.

exposed to imminent danger before the approach of morning.'[1]

For the first half of the eighteenth century, all the evidence leads to the impression that crime and disorder were much less prevalent in the rural districts and the provincial towns than in the Metropolis. The records of convictions at Quarter Sessions are relatively few and light. Such provincial newspapers as can still be consulted reveal no serious grievances in the way of the prevalence of robbery or assault. The impression of the country districts that we derive from many contemporary sources is that of a stolid, home-keeping and reasonably contented population; gross and sensual in its habits, but not incited to plunder or riot by extreme want; inclined occasionally to riot in resentment of this or that grievance, but saved by generous poor relief from destitution, and intellectually submissive to the justices of the peace. After the middle of the century the picture gradually changes for the worse. With the increase in vagrancy, coupled with the growth of passenger traffic and mails, there appears, on all the great roads, the professional highwayman. With the new and rapid growth of the Northern and Midland industrial centres, we find developing whole classes of local professional pickpockets and pilferers, swindlers, cheats, sharpers and 'scufflehunters' of every kind. The very growth of crowded slums in Liverpool and Manchester led to a reproduction on a smaller scale, of all the disorderly life of the Metropolis. 'Bodies of miscreants', we read of Chester in 1787, 'infest the

[1] *A Treatise on the Police of the Metropolis*, by Patrick Colquhoun, 1800, p. 2.

streets and rows early in the evenings, and insult with impunity, and lay under contribution whomsoever they meet. There are no watchmen, or others who can be applied to for redress.'[1] Towards the latter part of the century, the insidious but unmistakable worsening of the economic condition of the agricultural population, brought about by the enclosure of the commons and the rise in the cost of living, coupled with a spasmodic stringency in poor relief, is reflected in a general increase of rural delinquency. In 1786, we read of the West of England, 'Such depredations are committed in the different parts of the country by the horse and sheep stealers that the farmers are afraid to turn out their flocks into the fields. Within this week or two five horses have been carried off from the neighbourhood of Pendock in Worcestershire, and at different times within two years a gentleman farmer not far from thence has lost three score sheep.'[2] What seems to have been a sort of epidemic of rural crime is reported in 1788 at Pyrland, a village near Taunton (Somerset), on the estate of Sir William Yeo. 'Innumerable are the depredators and stealers of deer, sheep and fowls that have been already discovered. . . . Men, women and children have all been conspirators, and the whole country is in an uproar.We have strong evidence of twenty deer, and as many sheep, having been slaughtered and devoured in an old farmhouse belonging to Sir William Yeo. The chambers of this house are a perfect Golgotha, and horseloads of deer skins have been sold at a time from hence. Three or four years'

[1] *Gentleman's Magazine*, October 1787.
[2] *Bristol Gazette*, 13 July 1786.

wool was stolen out of the lofts over his stables, packed up in the open court, and carried off without interruption during his absence. The deer were killed early in the morning, if the baronet was at home, or shot openly in the middle of the day if absent. The sheep were mostly eaten by his out of door workmen and dependents, and five or six at a time have been driven away and sold, by persons of this description. . . . These thieves used to play at cards on their nights of feasting, and the stake to be played for was always declared, perhaps three or four turkeys, geese or ducks, &c., and the loser was to go forth and steal them against the next entertainment, or undergo punishment.'[1]

From the middle of the eighteenth century desperate mobs of destitute persons appear on the scene, enraged at one or other result of the Industrial Revolution. There were food-riots at Manchester in 1762, and others in Derbyshire in 1767.[2] We have already mentioned the spasm of insurrection of the Suffolk labourers in 1765, against the erection of Houses of Industry and the withdrawal of Outdoor Relief: an insurrection which caused the destruction of thousands of pounds worth of property, and was only put down, after more than a week's unrestrained licence, by a charge of dragoons. There were riots in Lancashire in 1779 'owing to the erection of certain mills and engines . . . for the manufacturing of cotton, which . . . tend to depreciate the price of labour'.[3] Sheffield

1 *Bristol Journal*, 8 March 1788.

2 *The Early English Cotton Industry*, by G. W. Daniels, 1920, p. 84.

3 MS. Minutes, Quarter Sessions, Lancashire, 11 November 1779; *Manchester Mercury*, 16 November 1779.

broke into revolt in 1791, in resentment of the enclosure of a large common. 'Hundreds of people assembled and [were] busily employed in pulling down the town gaol, after having given all the prisoners their liberty. From thence they went to Justice Wilkinson's house and set fire to his valuable library, but happily the fire was got under. They then set fire to seven large haystacks belonging to him, which are now in flames. . . . When the soldiers arrived they were obliged to fire several times. . . . The mob then dispersed. . . . The workmen are all in an uproar, and business of every kind is at a standstill.'[1] At Birmingham and other places, amid the terribly high prices of 1800, there were bread riots, against which the Yeomanry had to be called out, and a force of dragoons sent for. Between 1800 and 1810, when the press-gang was at work obtaining soldiers and sailors for the Napoleonic war, and County Benches were suppressing liquor licences and otherwise reforming the morals and manners of the lower orders,[2] there seems to have been a temporary diminution of riots and disorder. When again these break out, in 1811–12, and still more after the distressful year 1816, they show signs of being changed in character. The riots of the eighteenth century had been, almost exclusively, the mere impulses of an untamed people, born of their impatience of suffering or restraint, the habitual licentious disorder of the individuals gathering itself up from time to time into mob outrages on a large scale, excited by some local and temporary grievance

[1] *Public Advertiser*, 1 August 1791.

[2] *History of Liquor Licensing*, by S. and B. Webb, 1903, chap. iii, and the Appendix on the Movement for the Reformation of Manners.

—it might be the erection of a turnpike or the enclosure of a common, the introduction of a new machine or the establishment of a House of Industry, the scarcity of corn or the high prices of the butchers. There was, to put it briefly, in these eighteenth-century riots, no intermixture of sedition. From 1812 to 1832 a new spirit may be detected in the riots. They are still often wild protests against high prices or angry attacks on machinery. But instead of the eighteenth-century feeling of loyalty to the King and the Constitution, and the conviction that the grievances are innovations, there appears, practically for the first time, an unmistakable consciousness among the rioters, demonstrators, machine destroyers and rick burners, that what they are in rebellion against is the established order of society, laid down by Parliament, upheld by the Courts and enforced by the standing army.

Laying the Foundations of Democracy

These four main evils wrought by the Industrial Revolution in the environment of local institutions—the massing of men in urban districts, the devastating torrent of public nuisances, the catastrophic increase in destitution and pauperism, and the consequent prevalence of crime and sedition—had, as we indicated in the last chapter, completely undermined the old principles of government inherited from time immemorial and embodied in local custom, the Common Law and the Tudor and Stuart legislation. But the results of the Industrial Revolution were not exclusively iconoclastic. The pioneers of the new Capitalism were unwittingly laying the foundations of modern

Democracy. One of the barriers to reform, whether of national or of Local Government, was the Municipal Corporation, with its decaying groundwork of vocational organization, its oligarchical constitution, its trade privileges and monopolies, not to mention its representation in the House of Commons, its inveterate policy of excluding from citizenship, and frequently from employment, all those who did not belong to one or other of its original trade groups. It was exactly against the static exclusiveness of the old vocational basis of society that the new capitalists were waging a persistent, relentless and eventually successful war. Throughout the Northern and Midland Counties, the cotton manufacturers and the machine makers, the canal constructors and the colliery owners, were building up new communities, for the most part outside the area of any Municipal Corporation. If they were multiplying public nuisances, they were also defying the Lords of Manors; if they were massing men, women and children in mean streets and keeping them day and night in the works, they were also nullifying the Law of Settlement and enabling the poor to escape from the jurisdiction of the incumbent and the squire as Justices of the Peace. Above all, they were successfully posing as the only representatives of the consumers' desire for cheap and plentiful commodities. Moreover, it must not be forgotten that not all the displaced copyholders and independent handicraftsmen were pressed down into the sweated industrial proletariat. A not insignificant proportion of the more vigorous, self-controlled and acquisitive among them utilized their new economic freedom to make themselves foremen and managers, and even to become themselves millowners and capitalist *entrepreneurs*.

The universal freedom of competition and freedom of contract preached by Adam Smith and practised by the new capitalist industry were, in fact, liberating not only industrial, but also political energy. The very diversity of origin of the employers combined with their rise in economic power to make them reformers. It was from the class of the 'new rich', the manufacturers and warehousemen of Manchester, the shipowners and merchants of Liverpool, who found themselves excluded alike from the County Commission of the Peace and the Municipal Corporation, that emerged the most powerful recruits to the first stages of a movement towards political Democracy. Few of them, it is true, had, like Robert Owen and Francis Place, any sympathy with the industrial or political aspirations of the wage-earners. What they demanded was, in the phrase of the Liverpool reformers of 1830, 'equal privileges for all of equal station'. But it was from this essentially 'caste' struggle between the Tory squires and the Radical manufacturers that sprang, not only 'free trade in corn', the Factory Acts and an ever-widening Parliamentary franchise, but also, at successive removes, the general adoption throughout the whole Local Government of the Kingdom, of the modern Consumers' Democracy of universal suffrage.

But the Industrial Revolution unwittingly made an even greater contribution to the cause of industrial and political Democracy. The power-driven, machine-worked and ruthlessly managed establishments of the new industries produced, not only the sinews of war and the dominance of British enterprise in foreign markets, but also the British Trade Union Movement. 'Whilst industrial oppression belongs to all ages, it is not until the changing conditions of industry had reduced to an infinitesimal chance the journeyman's prospect of becoming himself a master, that we find the passage of ephemeral combinations into permanent trade societies.'[1] So long as all classes of the English people were divided up vertically into occupational groups, the majority of the families owning alike the instruments and the products of their labour, whether as agriculturists, as domestic manufacturers, or as town handicraftsmen, their economic aspirations and personal loyalties were attached to the leading members of the same occupational groups, even if these were their social superiors or economic exploiters. Hence we find, throughout the seventeenth century, the master craftsmen and the journeymen in each trade frequently supporting, by their petitions, the applications for privilege and monopoly made by the promoters of the national manufacturing and trading companies; whilst the copyholders and yeomen were always on the side of the rural landowners as against other sections of the community. This vocational bias was heightened by the instinctive Conservatism of the lower orders of the English people. The 'mob' of the eighteenth century, made up of the rabble from village and town, was invariably Tory in sympathy; and its violence was constantly directed against the reformers of the British constitution and the dissenters from the Established

[1] *History of Trade Unionism*, by S. and B. Webb, edition of 1920, p. 6.

Church. It is therefore not surprising that the early trade clubs of town artisans, and even the ephemeral combinations of factory operatives, instinctively turned first to the House of Commons and the Justices of the Peace for protection against the inroads made by the new Capitalism on the sufficiency and security of their livelihood. For some time, as we have described elsewhere,[1] the country gentleman of the House of Commons supported this appeal for the maintenance of the medieval and Tudor order; but towards the end of the eighteenth century, and especially during the financial strain of the Napoleonic war, the new industrial policy of unrestricted freedom of enterprise became almost universally accepted by the governing class. The abandonment of the operatives to the operation of free competition was even carried out with unflinching determination as a matter of principle. The Select Committee of the House of Commons in 1808 reported that the ancient legal protection of the workers' Standard of Life and security of employment was 'wholly inadmissible in principle, incapable of being reduced to practice by any means which can possibly be devised, and, if practicable, would be productive of the most fatal consequences'; and 'that the proposition relative to the limiting the number of apprentices is also entirely inadmissible, and would, if adopted by the House, be attended with the greatest injustice to the manufacturer as well as to the labourer'.[1] Needless to say, the governing class was by no

[1] Ibid., pp. 48–51.

[1] *Reports on Petitions of Cotton Weavers, 1809 and 1811*; quoted in *The History of Trade Unionism*, new edition, 1920, p. 56.

means impartial in the application of the new doctrines. Medieval regulation acted in restriction of free competition in the labour market not only to the pecuniary loss of the employers, but also to that of the employees, who, as the economists now see, could obtain the best terms for their labour only by collective instead of individual bargaining. Any such combination of the wage-earners, however, was in 1800 made more definitely than ever a criminal offence, which it took the organized workers the greater part of the nineteenth century wholly to abolish. We have traced elsewhere the gradual evolution of the Trade Union Movement during the past two hundred years, and its emergence into politics in the twentieth century, developing into the wider Labour Party of workers by hand or by brain, which is striving persistently to secure, for the community that 'lives by working', as contrasted with the still dominant section that 'lives by owning', such a Parliamentary majority as would enable it to constitute the government of the country. This brings us a long way from the slow and gradual rise of the new capitalist industry, from the latter part of the seventeenth century onward. But it is not too much to say that it was the sweeping away by the Industrial Revolution of the peasant copyholder, the domestic manufacturer and the independent craftsman, that made possible the transformation of the bulk of English people into a horizontally stratified democracy of workers, claiming alike industrial and political control for those who constitute the great majority of the community.

The New Conceptions of Political Liberty and Personal Freedom

It will always be a matter of dispute how far the Industrial Revolution, with its novel ideas of free competition and free contract, was itself the result of the new conceptions of personal freedom and political liberty that may be traced in the rise of religious Nonconformity, and that were so dramatically manifested in, and so widely advertised by the American Declaration of Independence and the French Revolution. Whilst some eminent thinkers, like Burke, combined an almost fanatical adhesion to the existing political order with a naïve credulity in the beneficence of free competition, there were many disciples of Adam Smith who welcomed alike the success of the American Rebellion and the sweeping political changes inaugurated by the French Revolution. At the end of the eighteenth century there seemed to be no incompatibility between complete political Democracy and the unrestrained exercise of property rights in everything that could possibly be made subject to private ownership. In the seventeenth century there had been, we think, a clearer vision. In those illuminating debates in the Council of War at Reading in 1647, we watch Cromwell and Ireton spending day after day in trying to persuade their officers and men 'That which is most radicall and fundamentall, and which if you take away there is noe man hath any land, any goods, [or] any civill interest, that is this: that those that chuse the Representors for the making of Lawes by which this State and Kingedome are to bee govern'd, are the persons who, taken together, doe comprehend the locall interest of this Kingedome; that is, the persons in whome all land lies, and those in Corporations in whome all trading lies. . . . If wee shall goe to take away this fundamentall parte of the civill constitution, wee shall plainly goe to take away all property and interest that any man hath, either in land by inheritance, or in estate by possession, or any thinge else.'[1] And they defended their proposal of excluding from the Parliamentary suffrage all men without landed property or corporate privileges, by comparing them to foreigners who come to live in the Kingdom, having no permanent interest in it. It was useless for the protagonist of the other party, Colonel Rainborow, to assert 'I doe nott finde anythinge in the law of God, that a Lord shall chuse twenty Burgesses, and a Gentleman butt two, or a poore man shall chuse none. I finde noe such thinge in the law of nature, nor in the law of nations. Butt I doe finde, that all Englishmen must bee subject to English lawes, and I doe verily beleive, that there is noe man butt will say, that the foundation of all law lies in the people. . . . Therefore I doe [think] and am still of the same opinion; that every man born in England cannot, ought nott, neither by the law of God nor the law of nature, to bee exempted from the choice of those who are to make lawes, for him to live under, and for him, for ought I know, to loose his life under.'[2]

[1] *The Clarke Papers: Selections from the Papers of William Clarke*, edited by C. H. Firth, for the Camden Society, 1891, vol. i, pp. 302–3. And see *English Democratic Ideas in the Seventeenth Century*, by G. P. Gooch, pp. 202–6.

[2] *The Clarke Papers: Selections from the Papers of William Clarke*, edited by C. H. Firth, for the Camden Society, 1891, vol. i, pp. 304–5.

Again and again Cromwell and Ireton reiterate that if 'one man hath an equall right with another to the chusing of him that shall governe him—by the same right of nature, hee hath an equal right in any goods he sees: meate, drinke, cloathes, to take and use them for his sustenance. . . . If the Master and servant shall bee equall Electors, then clearlie those that have noe interest in the Kingedome will make itt their interest to chuse those that have noe interest. Itt may happen, that the majority may, by law, nott in a confusion, destroy propertie; there may bee a law enacted, that there shall bee an equality of goods and estate.'[1] At last Colonel Rainborow ironically retorts: 'Sir I see, that itt is impossible to have liberty butt all propertie must be taken away. If itt be laid downe for a rule, and if you will say itt, itt must bee soe.'[2]

No such foreboding of the economic implications of Political Democracy hampered the leaders of either the American or the French Revolution. In the Continental Congress of 1776 the founders of the United States saw no contradiction in terms between the institution of slavery and the declaration 'that all men are created equal; that they are endowed by their Creator with certain inalienable rights, and among these are life, liberty and the pursuit of happiness'. It is accordingly not surprising to find Hamilton and Jefferson alike without any inkling of a possible incompatibility between a universal equality of individual liberty and the tacit inclusion of land and other instruments of

[1] *The Clarke Papers: Selections from the Papers of William Clarke*, vol. i, p. 307.
[2] Ibid., p. 315.

production among the things in which private property was to be maintained and ensured.[1] A few years later the French revolutionists could unhesitatingly assume that an absolute right of private property, without limits or qualifications, was actually implicit in the 'Rights of Man', and in political citizenship. 'The end of all political association', declared the French National Assembly in 1789, 'is the preservation of the natural and imprescriptible rights of man; and these rights are Liberty, Property, Security and Resistance of Oppression.' The explanation of this common lack of appreciation of the American and the French revolutionaries, as of the economic optimism of the Adam Smith of 1776, is to be found in the fact that the full results of the Industrial Revolution on the practical freedom of the individual wage-earner had not then revealed themselves. In the United States, where land was still to be had for the asking, and any but the smallest capitals were nonexistent, the fullest 'Individualism' was as practicable in the production of subsistence as in political association. The French cultivator was conscious of political oppression, but not yet of Capitalism as itself depriving him of freedom. The taxation and personal servitude to which he was subjected came, not from his being ousted from his fragment of a communal ownership of the land, but from the arbitrary exactions of his *seigneur*, together with the *gabelle* and other direct imposts of the Government. The labourers, who had swelled the population

[1] For Hamilton's special sense of the importance of giving influence to property, see *The Federalist*, No. 54 (p. 364 of Ford's edition).

of the little market towns, as of Paris itself, saw their enemies not in the capitalist employer, but in the restrictions of the obsolescent *jurandes* or of the antiquated Municipal Authorities, by which the newcomers, or the unapprenticed man, or indeed anyone outside the privileged circles, was prevented from obtaining remunerative employment. In the contemporary England, too, 'the country', Thomas Paine could declare, 'is cut up into monopolies. Every chartered town is an aristocratical monopoly in itself, and the qualification of electors proceeds out of those chartered monopolies. Is this what Mr. Burke means by a constitution? In these chartered monopolies, a man coming from another part of the country is hunted from them as if he were a foreign enemy. An Englishman is not free of his own country: every one of those places presents a barrier in his way, and tells him he is not a freeman, that he has no rights. Within these monopolies are other monopolies. In a city, such for instance as Bath, which contains between twenty and thirty thousand inhabitants, the right of electing representatives to Parliament is monopolized into about thirty-one persons. And within these monopolies are still others. A man, even of the same town, whose parents were not in circumstances to give him an occupation, is debarred, in many cases, from the natural right of acquiring one, be his genius or industry what it may.'[1]

It was therefore inevitable that, with all these

[1] *Rights of Man*, by Thomas Paine, 1791; included in his *Political Works*, 1819, vol. i, p. 46. See also Godwin's *Political Justice*.

personal oppressions, these municipal and vocational monopolies, these hampering restrictions on men earning a livelihood as they best could, that the whole strength of the reform movement should have been directed to the removal of what were obviously 'artificial' restrains on individual freedom. The twin movements for political and industrial freedom seemed to be but parts of a common bursting of bonds. Thus, the constant aspiration of the revolutionaries of the close of the eighteenth century, alike in England and in France, was to get back to the individual, the common citizen, the undifferentiated man. Parcelled out into equal electoral districts so that each man should count as one, and for no more than any other man, this mass of identical citizens were to elect their representatives and thereby control their agents, in the indispensable work of government. Thus, the undifferentiated citizen, whose needs the government was to serve, and whose freedom in disposing of his income was to be absolute, was visualized, not as a producer, whether lawyer or land cultivator, cleric or craftsman, physician or farrier, but entirely as a consumer of commodities and services. It was this particular conception of political liberty and personal freedom that was one of the ferments that in England determined the new principles of Local Government presently to be described.

At this point in our analysis of the new mental environment of English Local Government between the Revolution and the Municipal Corporations Act we are brought against religious Nonconformity and its rapid spread, especially among the industrial workers of the North and Midlands, during the latter part of this period. With the theological and emotional aspects of this revolutionary movement of thought we are not here concerned. For our present purpose it counts merely as one among many expressions of the new conceptions of political liberty and personal freedom. Perhaps the most bitterly resented manifestations of the oligarchical principle was the exclusion of Dissenters from all offices of power and dignity, alike in the Counties and in the Municipal Corporations: an exclusion actually sanctioned by statute law. On the other hand, the humbler and more onerous offices of Overseer, Constable and Surveyor of Highways, and, oddly enough, also that of Churchwarden, were, as we have shown, obligatory on all inhabitants not expressly granted a privileged exemption. Moreover, it was always in the power of a select body recruited by co-option to exclude Nonconformists even from membership, as well as from all offices whatsoever, and, this as we have shown, was the invariable practice of the Select Vestries of Bristol and London. Hence, even the wealthy shipowners and merchants of Liverpool and the millowners and warehousemen of Manchester, the shopkeepers of St. James's and St. Marylebone, if, as was frequently the case, they did not belong to the Anglican Church, found themselves, like the Roman Catholics, not only excluded from public office, but actually taxed and governed by trade rivals who happened to adhere to the established creed. It was, more than anything else, this ostracism because of their religion that made these opulent reformers so persistent in their demand, as expressed in the Liverpool petition, that 'all in equal station should enjoy equal privileges'.[1] In the new manufacturing districts in which the Nonconformists were in the majority they sometimes took their revenge. We have described in our account of the open Vestry[2] the turbulent public meetings in the ancient Parish churches of Leeds and Manchester, when Nonconformist Churchwardens, even occasionally with their hats on, whilst smoking their pipes, sitting on the Communion table, objected to such items in the Parish accounts as payment for the sacramental wine and the washing of surplices; and refused resolutely, amid the applause of a disorderly mob, to make any Church Rate. Beneath the rivalry of religious creeds we see emerging the contemporary struggle between government by the minority who performed the service, and government by the mass of undifferentiated citizens who were assumed to enjoy it.[3]

The Utilitarians

The impulse to change supplied by the common faith in political liberty and personal freedom, and the emphasis laid on satisfying the desires of the average citizen-consumer, were greatly strengthened, from the end of the eighteenth century, by the persuasive force

[1] *The Manor and the Borough*, p. 701.

[2] *The Parish and the County*, pp. 91–103.

[3] The three rival conceptions of government, by the vocation concerned, by political democracy, and by consumers' democracy, can be followed in the history of the Christian churches. Whilst the Roman Catholic Church is a purely vocational government, most of the English nonconformist denominations are unmixed consumers' democracies. The Church of England presents a mixed government of vocational and political control, to which has been added by recent legislation, a certain degree of congregational or consumers' participation.

of a new social philosophy. The Utilitarians, as Professor Graham Wallas remarks in his admirable *Life of Francis Place*, 'though they broke with the French revolutionary thinkers and the whole doctrine of Natural Rights, nevertheless retained many of the characteristic habits of eighteenth-century thought. They believed themselves to have found a common-sense philosophy, by which ordinary selfish men could be convinced that the interests of each invariably coincided with the interests, if not of all, at any rate, of the majority.'[1] What was needed to complete this all-embracing principle of individual self-interest was knowledge, by which term Jeremy Bentham and James Mill meant, not the observation and analysis of facts, but a series of logically accurate deductions from a single law of human nature, namely that every man will follow his own interests as he understands them: a law as certain and as uniform in its operation in human society as the law of gravitation in the physical universe. 'So complete was my father's reliance on the influence of reason over the mind of mankind,' we are told by John Stuart Mill in his *Autobiography*, 'whenever it is allowed to reach them, that he felt as if all would be gained if the whole population were taught to read, if all sorts of opinions were allowed to be addressed to them, by word and in writing, and if, by the means of the suffrage, they could nominate a legislature to give effect to the opinions they adopted.'[2]

It was plain that this choice by every man of the

[1] *Life of Francis Place*, by Graham Wallas, 1898, p. 89.

[2] John Stuart Mill's *Autobiography*, p. 106; *The Life of Francis Place*, by Graham Wallas, 1898, p. 93.

pursuit of his own interests was, in the England of George the Third, hampered and prevented by all sorts of obsolete and ill-contrived laws, as well as by institutions devised for the purpose of giving exceptional advantages to favoured classes and individuals. Accordingly, Bentham[1] and his disciples, here following Jefferson and Priestley, were perpetually emphasizing the fact that any social institution, even the British Constitution itself, ought to be swept away if it ceased to be useful; that is, if it could be shown not to conduce to the greatest good of the greatest number. Hence all laws ought to be periodically reviewed and suitably amended, or even replaced by entirely new laws according to the circumstances of the time. The old plea in favour of local customs, 'that they had existed from time immemorial', or the claim that the Common Law of England must be maintained because it embodied the wisdom of past generations, appeared to Jeremy Bentham and James Mill as a pernicious superstition. It was at this point that the Utilitarians found themselves in practical agreement with those who believed, with fanatical fervour, in the 'Rights of Man'. The most vital of the three fundamental Rights of Man, Dr. Price had explained in his famous sermon

[1] We need not refer the student to Bentham's *Works*, in Sir John Bowring's edition in 11 volumes. Much suggestive analysis of the influence and significance of the Utilitarians will be found in Sir Leslie Stephen's *The English Utilitarians* as in the *Life of Francis Place* and other works by Professor Graham Wallas. But we have found most illuminating, in connexion with Local Government, the three brilliant volumes, by M. Elie Halevy, on *La Formation du Radicalisme économique* (*La Jeunesse de Bentham*, 1901; *L'Évolution du doctrine utilitaire*, 1901; and *Le Radicalisme philosophique*, 1904).

on the fourth of November, 1789, were to choose our own governors, to cashier them for misconduct, and to frame a government for ourselves.[1] These rights, it is clear, involved a freedom of perpetual innovation on the part of each succeeding generation. 'The reasonableness and propriety of things', declared Thomas Paine in 1792, 'must be examined abstractly from custom and usage; and in this point of view, the right which grows into practice today is as much a right, and as old in principle and theory, as if it had the customary sanction of a thousand ages. . . . It is, however, certain', he continued, 'that the opinions of men, with respect to systems and principles of government, are changing fast in all countries. The alteration in England, within the space of little more than a year, is far greater than could then have been believed, and it is daily and hourly increasing. It moves along the country with the silence of thought.'[2]

The effect of the Utilitarian social philosophers was thus not only to discredit local custom and the Common Law, and to lead to the enactment of brand new statutes, and their constant revision and codification, but also to suggest new principles of administration. For, although the Utilitarians firmly believed that each person always acted in such a way as he believed would increase his own pleasures or diminish his own pains,

[1] *A Discourse on the Love of our Country*, delivered on 4 November before the Society for Commemorating the Revolution in Great Britain, 1789, by Robert Price, D.D., LL.D., F.R.S., London, 1789.

[2] *Letter Addressed to the Addressers, on the late Proclamation*, by Thomas Paine, 1792, included in his *Political Works*, 1819, vol. ii, p. 34.

Bentham never had as much faith as Adam Smith in the assurance that this free play of individual self-interest would automatically, without social contrivances of one sort or another, produce the greatest happiness of the greatest number. Accordingly, unlike Adam Smith, Bentham was constantly devising new laws and new social institutions to replace the old ones. Never has there been, at any time or in any country, such a stream of projects for deliberate and often compulsory social improvement, as issued from the little house near Birdcage Walk, whether in the way of amendments of the Poor Law, the institution of reformatory prisons, the collective organization of 'Schools for All', the reorganization of the magistracy and the Courts of Justice, the codification of the law, so that it might be brought within the knowledge of every citizen, and the most ingenious social devices for systematically preventing error, fraud, misunderstanding or deceit. All these separate projects had in common the idea of artificially combining the pecuniary self-interest of the individual citizen with the greatest happiness of the greatest number. Far from dispensing with law and public administration, what Bentham desired was that his uncouth formula, 'the duty-and-interest-junction-principle', should dominate the whole field of government, which he always recognized as indispensable. This explains his obsession in favour of 'farming', or putting out to contract, at the lowest price yielded by competitive tender, every function in which this plan was conceivable, whether the execution of public works, the conduct of a prison, the setting to work of the unemployed, or even the maintenance of orphan children. But he could not ignore the fact that the contractor would himself seek his own pecuniary advantage; and to prevent this militating against the public interest, Bentham devised an equally bewildering array of checks, from the 'central inspection chamber', perpetually surveying the radiating corridors and workshops of the Panopticon, to the 'life-warranting principle', by which the prison or Poor Law 'farmer' had to pay a forfeit, at a progressive rate, for every death above the previous average that took place among those committed to his charge. All this, as subsequently elaborated by Edwin Chadwick, involved a hierarchy of centrally appointed inspectors, to whose pecuniary advantage it would be to 'catch out' the army of contractors. In short, Bentham sought, as would now be said by the business man, to introduce into government departments the motives and methods of profit-making enterprise. His influence, exercised through his disciples, and notably in the couple of decades of Edwin Chadwick's official life, was to 'commercialize' public administration.

There was another implication of the Benthamite philosophy which had a special bearing on English Local Government. As what had to be secured was the interest of the majority of the whole community, it seemed to follow that no geographical section of the community, and therefore no Local Authority, could be trusted or permitted to enjoy complete autonomy in the interests of its own constituents. We forget today how novel a hundred years ago was the inference that, not only general laws applicable to the whole nation, but also central government departments able to secure the interests of the community as a whole, even against the desires of any one locality, were imperatively required. The Benthamites foresaw that these central departments at Whitehall would have, for their function, by their ubiquitous inspection and continuous instructions, to overcome the 'froward retention of custom', the bucolic ignorance, the secretiveness, the bias, and the possible corruption characterizing remote districts, small areas of administration, and any 'localized' or 'sectional' group. Hence a commercialized municipal administration was to be incessantly stimulated, guided and checked, under the control of the national Representative Assembly, by an authoritative expert bureaucracy. It is easy, after a century of experience, to see defects and limitations in the elaborate official reconstruction that formed an indispensable part of the Benthamite scheme. It was characteristic of the extreme intellectualism of the Benthamites that they vastly exaggerated the superiority in width of information, extent of experience, and knowledge of principles, which a central government might be expected to possess as compared with any Local Authority; just as they enormously over-estimated the certainty with which the able investigators and distinguished administrators of the central departments could be trusted to decide what were the interests of the community as a whole; or the persuasiveness with which they could induce a recalcitrant Local Authority to believe in the superiority of Whitehall. We may today recognize how much there is to be said for a more highly organized and more delicately adjusted relation, and for a more balanced estimate of the claims and wills of local and central authorities respectively, than Bentham ever visualized or than Chadwick would admit. But no one who realizes the state of things in 1833, when under the Reformed Parliament, the Benthamites, for a few brief years, came into their own, can doubt the great public benefit, even with all their shortcomings and defects, effected by the Commissioners who inquired into the Poor Law, the Municipal Corporations, and the sanitary condition of the population; or the imperative necessity of some such central departments as they wished to see established to inspect, guide and control the local administration of poor relief, public health and municipal government generally.

The New Principles in Local Government

We have now to trace the emergence, amid the revolutionary changes both in the industrial environment and in thought, between the Revolution and the Great Reform Bill, of new principles in Local Government. These new principles are found embodied, not only in the succession of Parliamentary statutes culminating in the Poor Law Amendment Act, the Municipal Corporations Act and the Acts for registering Births, Deaths and Marriages, but also in the administrative expedients spontaneously adopted by the Parish and the County, the Municipal Corporations and the new Statutory Authorities for Special Purposes.

The more important of these new conceptions were in direct contradiction of the old principles that they superseded. The use of the contractor, employing labour at competitive wages, gradually ousted the citizen's obligation to serve gratuitously in public office, and introduced the ratepayer as the predominant economic interest in Local Government. Government by citizen-consumers superseded the decaying remnants of the vocational organization that underlay the constitution of the Manor and the Borough. Representative Democracy gradually gained ground on, though it never entirely eliminated, the oligarchical principle of Co-option. The advent of the salaried expert, bringing the technique required for the new services, threatened the authority, if not the very existence, of the inheritor or purchaser of freehold office, endowed with the right to rule or to tax his fellow-citizens. Equally important with these changes, in the very structure and function of the local institutions, was the increasing intervention of Parliament, prescribing the constitution and powers of local governing bodies, with the resulting substitution of innovating statutes for immemorial local custom and the Common Law. Finally, in the supervising, inspecting and sanctioning authority vested in central government departments, there is the beginning of a new kind of national executive control of local affairs. The only conception that was, down to the very end of the period, retained almost intact, was that which made property, if possible landed property, a necessary qualification for important public office, thereby maintaining the landed gentry as the Rulers of the County; though their activities were increasingly encroached upon by new forms of Ratepayers' Democracies.'[1]

[1] It is significant of the slow and gradual evolution of English institutions that, in 1922, after nearly another century

The Contractor and His Staff of Wage Labourers

When the task of Local Government became too onerous for the unpaid and compulsorily serving officer of the Parish or Manor, Borough or County; when the work to be done involved the continuous labour, day after day, not of one but of a number of pairs of hands; when even the planning and direction of the operation transcended both the time and the skill of the farmer or tradesman conscripted for his turn of service as Overseer, or that of the country gentleman called upon to act as Bridgemaster, recourse was had to the paid service of the contractor, with his staff of men at wages. At the outset, this new expedient was far removed from the nineteenth century professional profit-maker wielding armies of workmen of different kinds and grades. The first innovation was no more considerable than to permit the Churchwarden or Surveyor of Highways, the Town Clerk or Bridgemaster to make payments to one or more workmen, who could carry out the necessary repairs or works at the customary rates. Presently the whole service was entrusted to a master-craftsman or local trader, who might or might not assume the title of Town Carpenter or Pavior, but who was habitually employed, either by the Local Authority itself, or successively by individual citizens, to do what was required in building or paving. As the business grew, in variety as well as in magnitude, and especially when the needs to be met were those of a new and rapidly

of extensive changes, we find still in existence many isolated survivals of all the old principles that characterized the institutions of the close of the seventeenth century.

growing urban district, there came to be a whole set of tradesmen employed on various kinds of building and sewer work, on the multitudinous repairs of the increasing public property of one kind or another, and on the furnishing or decorating of the different institutions. Meanwhile, the habit of contracting for public services had been growing along another line. Up and down the country, in every conceivable service, the easiest way of getting done any continuous duty, seemed to be to 'farm' it, or put it out to contract to the man who offered the most advantageous terms. It is the almost universal prevalence of this contract system in the eighteenth century that explains the exiguity of the executive staff. The stretch of highway could be repaired and kept in order by a contractor. The troublesome accumulation of garbage could be kept down by getting someone to contract for its removal, with no more demand on the time or labour of the unpaid public officers than the periodical payment of the 'farmer's' account. The rows on rows of street lamps, which took the place of the swinging lantern of the indivual householder, could be made and fixed by contract, cleaned by contract and lit by contract. The collection of the public revenue could equally be 'farmed'; and tolls and dues, from parish pounds and manorial cornmills up to municipal markets and turnpike roads, could be made the basis of contractual payments, leaving the contractor to incur all the labour and risk which would otherwise have fallen on the Local Authority or its gratuitously serving officers. It was early discovered that the poor could be 'farmed', and their maintenance secured, either for so much per head, or even for a fixed lump sum per annum, the 'farmer' making what profit he could out of 'setting the poor to work'. Having got under his control the contingent of pauper labour, the contractor could then profitably tender for the service of cleaning the streets at a fixed sum. But the most scandalous of all these forms of contract, because of the opportunity and the temptation that it gave for the worst oppressions, was the farming of the prisons. These, like the workhouses, could be let by contract to the gaolers, keepers, masters or governors; the wretched inmates, if fed and clothed at all, could be fed and clothed by contract, and even physicked by contract. The vagrants were conveyed by contract, fed by contract and also whipped by contract; and when the felons were sent beyond seas, they were habitually transported by contract, and sold by auction on arrival to those who contracted at the highest rate to employ them.

Now, this substitution, as the motive and reward for the execution of the function of the Local Authority, of profit making and the earning of wages for public work—inevitable as it may have been—had all sorts of far-reaching results, upon which it is unnecessary here to dwell. But one of its accompaniments, in the very rudimentary stage at which government organization had then arrived, was an unchecked, and, indeed, an entirely unashamed prevalence of what is now stigmatized as favouritism and corruption. When the holder of a public office was allowed to make its exercise an opportunity for private profit, it became almost inevitable that his interests as a profit-maker should come into conflict with his duty as a vigilant steward of the public funds. When the jobs to be paid for by the Parish or the Borough were given, as a matter of course, to the uncontrolled Parish Officers or to the various members of the Select Vestry or of the Town Council, or even when they were shared among a relatively small body of Freemen, without competition and without any impertinent scrutiny of their bills, the way was clear for the orgy of corruption which characterized, in varying degrees, nearly all the Local Government of the eighteenth and early nineteenth centuries. The very exclusiveness inherent in the dominant principle of Co-option, as a method of recruiting the governing group, accelerated the downward drift into favouritism and corruption. 'Every Parish Officer', wrote a shrewd London observer in 1796, 'thinks he has a right to make a round bill on the Parish during his year of power. An apothecary physics the poor; a glazier, first in cleaning, breaks the church windows, and afterwards mends them, or at least charges for it; a painter repairs the Commandments, puts new coats on Moses and Aaron, gilds the organ-pipes, and dresses the little Cherubim about the loft as fine as vermilion, Prussian blue, and Dutch gold can make them. The late Churchwardens [of the writer's own London Parish] were a silversmith and a woollen draper; the silversmith new-fashioned the communion plate, and the draper new-clothed the pulpit and put fresh curtains to the windows.'[1] It would, however, be unfair to suggest that predominantly Tory membership of the Close Bodies was any worse at this game than the

[1] *The Olio*, by Francis Grose, 1796, pp. 217–18; *The Parish and the County*, p. 79.

predominantly Radical and popularly elected Common Councillors of the City of London. The most common form of plunder, in which nearly all the members of that Corporation participated, was the execution of work or the provision of goods for the Corporation in their respective trades, without competition, often at the most extravagant prices. 'Here the sacred office of a Common Councilman', we are told by a contemporary writer, 'is prostituted to the lowest and basest ends.'[1] The multiplication of standing or permanent master craftsmen undertaking work as profit-making contractors for the Corporation was carried on, we are told by a contemporary writer, 'to an incorrigible extent'. There was the 'Land Carpenter of the Bridge House, the Water Carpenter, the Bridge House Mason, the Bridge House Bricklayer, the City Plasterer, the City Plumber, the Bridge House Plumber, the City and Bridge House Painter, the City Printer, the City and Bridge House Glazier, the City Stationer, the City Smith, the Bridge House Smith, the City Founder, the City and Bridge House Purveyor,' and so on, *ad infinitum*.[2] Spasmodic attempts were made by the more honourable members of the Court to prevent the grossest of the favouritism by Standing Orders, which it cost a whole half-century of effort to get adopted, designed to stop the habitual practice of the shopkeeper members giving each other orders for supplies or work, or actually appointing each other to the salaried offices in their gift. Unfortunately the

[1] *City Corruption and Maladministration Displayed*, by a Citizen, 1738, p. 4; *The Manor and the Borough*, p. 650.
[2] Ibid.

Standing Orders could always be suspended; and we are told by a newspaper critic in 1826 that this course was habitually taken. 'Whenever a case arises in which they ought to be strictly enforced, some Honourable Member rises in his place and moves that they be suspended, and, as a matter of course, they are suspended accordingly. . . . Whenever any snug situation . . . is declared vacant . . . any member of the Court . . . persuades some kind friend . . . to move that in his particular case the Standing Orders may be suspended. . . . The Court finds it impossible to resist an appeal of this kind, as it is made on the principle, "Do this for me today, and I will do as much for you another time".'[1]

To the modern administrator it must seem strange that not for something like a century is there any systematic attempt to prevent this naïve combination of profit-making with public office. The eighteenth century does not seem to have been able to bring itself to give up the plan of gratuitously serving public officers, constrained to undertake onerous duties. Even in the nineteenth century the engagement of a salaried official staff was commonly denounced—as it still occasionally is in the twentieth century—as 'bureaucracy'. The first remedy for corruption was an attempt to restrain the unpaid representative, whose duty it was to protect the common purse, from himself contracting for public work. Not until the last decades of the eighteenth century do Parish Vestries decide, in one form or another, 'that none of the gentlemen

[1] No. 629 of 'Sketches of Aldermen, etc.' (MSS. Guildhall Library); *The Manor and the Borough*, p. 651.

hereafter chosen and appointed to the offices of Churchwardens and Overseers of the Poor of this Parish shall, under any pretence whatever, be permitted to serve the workhouse with provisions, or any other article or commodity whatsoever, or send any materials, or do any work either in or about the workhouse, or otherwise on the Parish account while in office'.[1] It occurred to someone to embody such a self-denying ordinance in statute law, and this was effected in some of the Local Acts.[2] Not until 1782 was it made a penal offence for Churchwardens or Overseers, or other persons responsible for the maintenance or management of the poor, themselves to contract for, or supply, goods to be paid for out of the public funds for which they were themselves responsible.[3] In 1824 a similar prohibition was applied to members of Turnpike Trusts.[4] Even then no general statute forbade a member of a Municipal Corporation, or, indeed, a member of any Local Authority not being a Turnpike Trust, and not concerned with poor relief, to supply goods to, or do work for, or enter into profitable contracts with the corporate body of which he formed part. Not until the Municipal Corporations Act of 1835, and then only

[1] *The Parish and the County*, p. 120.

[2] It seems that in one of the Local Acts obtained by the City of London in the first half of the eighteenth century, the House of Commons insisted, against the wishes of the representatives of the Common Council, on inserting a clause excluding members of the Common Council from participating in any of the contracts under it (*The Manor and the Borough*, p. 650). Exactly when similar clauses became the rule in Local Acts we have not been able to discover.

[3] In the so-called Gilbert Act of 1782 (22 George III, c. 83, sec. 42).

[4] 3 George IV, c. 126, c. 65 (General Turnpike Act, 1824).

with regard to the Boroughs to which that Act applied, was this even made a cause of disqualification for office.[1]

At the beginning of the nineteenth century, the Philosophic Radicals and Political Economists thought they had found an additional or an alternative remedy in the universal insistence on competitive tendering, and the automatic acceptance of the lowest tender.[2] This unredeemed competitive tendering, when it was not defeated by 'rings' and 'knock-outs', such as those constantly resorted to by the farmers of turnpike tolls, when these were put up to auction, led to a steady degradation, alike in the quality of the workmanship or the efficiency of the service, and in the rates of wages paid to the unorganized crowds of labourers by whom the manual work was done. Whatever may have been the immediate pecuniary saving to the ratepayer, the moral results were disastrous. It is not too much to say that the ubiquitous introduction of the profit-making contractor, intent, on the one

[1] 5 & 6 William IV, c. 76, sec. 28 (Municipal Corporations Act, 1835); extended to contracts for the borough gaol by 7 William IV, and 1 Victoria, c. 78, sec. 39.

[2] It is remarkable that not until 1819 was any power given generally to Parishes to appoint a salaried officer to perform the duties of Overseer (59 George III, c. 12). By 1834 this power had been acted upon chiefly in the urban districts of the North of England, there being then 267 Assistant Overseers in Lancashire and 205 in Yorkshire (Third Annual Report of Poor Law Commissioners, 1837, p. 21). The Poor Law Commissioners, in their early years, prided themselves on putting out, by competitive tendering, even the medical attendance on the sick poor; in some cases even prescribing a maximum sum which could not be exceeded, however numerous might be the poor on whom the Medical Officer was required to attend.

hand, upon buying labour in the cheapest market, even in the workhouse or the prison, and on the other, upon extracting from the public authority, by fair means or foul, the highest possible price—evoking, as the system did, among the sweated workers, a like desire to do as little labour as possible, without regard to the efficiency of the service—has left, even today, an evil tradition of inefficiency and greed in the lower branches of municipal work.

The Coming of the Ratepayer

The abandonment of the obligatory and gratuitous service of the ordinary citizen in public office involved the establishment of the 'cash nexus' as the basis of all the transactions of the Local Authority. For it is clear that the payment of an evergrowing volume of salaries and wages, if not also of contractor's profits, meant the raising of a corresponding money revenue, which took the form of a periodical levy of leys, cesses, scots or rates on all the occupiers of land or buildings. We cannot here explore the innumerable ramifications, in the course of the past hundred years, of this substitution of taxation upon every householder all the time for personal service by a minority of citizens in rotation. From it have sprung all the intricate problems of the economic incidence of local taxation upon different classes of citizens, different kinds of property and different forms of industry. To the same root may be traced the financial expedients of loans for short periods and long, the subsidizing of some municipal services out of the profits made in others, and the necessity of 'equalizing' the burdens of the various

Local Authorities by subventions from the National Exchequer. Another result of far-reaching importance, and one which was already beginning to be manifested at the opening of the nineteenth century, was the new cleavage of interest between those citizens who felt themselves directly benefited by this or that municipal service, and those who were conscious only of paying for it in new and onerous taxation. This cleavage already appears in the objections of the turbulent Democracy, which swarmed into the open Vestries, to the expenditure on the new safeguards and amenities of urban life desired by the more substantial citizens. The mass of wage-earning labourers of Plymouth Dock [now Devonport] vehemently protested in 1813 against being saddled with the payment of new rates for 'lamping, lighting and watching the town of Dock, the enormous expense of which they deprecate and see no necessity for. . . . The population of this Parish will consist principally of persons employed in His Majesty's Dockyard. . . . Mechanics and the labouring classes . . . will amount to about seven or eight in ten of the inhabitants, whose employments are of that nature as to call them early to bed and early to rise; and consequently partaking in no one degree of the benefits of a measure towards which they will be called upon materially to contribute; with respect to their property it may be said in a general way that it does not consist of more than they themselves are able to protect.'[1] It is not necessary to comment on the analogous cleavage,

[1] MS. Minutes, Stoke Damarel Vestry [now Devonport], 10 October and 14 November 1813; *Municipal Origins*, by F. H. Spencer, 1911, p. 33–34.

a hundred years later, which leads to the constant struggle, in the Local Government of today, of the class that resents having to pay rates for schools which its own children do not use, for maternity and child welfare institutions which its own families do not require, and for the healthy maintenance of the unemployed workmen and their dependents, in whom the upper and middle class have no interest.

There were, however, two immediate consequences of the steady increase of Local Government based on local taxation, which began, even in the eighteenth century, to perplex the local administrators. The fact that every householder had to contribute towards the cost of every step taken by the Parish or the County, the Improvement Commissioners or the Borough, and that the benefits of such action were enjoyed in common, emphasized the position of the Local Authority as being, virtually, an Association of Consumers, in which membership was obligatory and universal. It seemed to follow, as a necessary corollary—at least to those who believed that Representation and Taxation should always be united—that the ratepayers were entitled to elect and to control all those who spent the ratepayers' money.

Government as an Association of Consumers

We pause here to consider what seems to us one of the most interesting questions in the natural history of institutions, namely at what stage and at what date did government begin to appear as predominantly an Association of Consumers. There is much to be said for the contention that all the governmental institutions in olden time were rooted in the assumption that the persons concerned had a common vocation, or at least a common right to exercise a particular function, to render a particular service or to produce a particular product. And, broadly speaking, it was to the vocation itself, whatever its constitution, that was committed the direction of its activities. That is to say, the Manor and the Municipal Corporation, and even the landowners who as Justices of the Peace ruled the Counties—like the King and his warriors, the Church and its priesthood, such nascent professions as the lawyers and the medical men, the chartered National Companies for overseas trade or for mining or other monopolies at home, and, last but not least, the Merchant and Craft Gilds—were all of the nature of Associations of Producers. It is scarcely too much to say that, in connexion with anything like the exercise of governmental functions, so far as our limited researches have gone, we do not come upon the conception of an Association of Consumers until the close of the seventeenth century. Even in that century, as we have shown, and for long afterwards, it was upon the decaying remnants of vocational organization that continued to rest the constitutional structure and the authority of the Manorial Courts, the Municipal Corporations and, we may almost say, Quarter Sessions itself. There remains to be considered the Parish, upon the nature and antiquity of which there has been much controversy, based, as we think, upon inadequate historical knowledge. Whether it is at all true, as Toulmin Smith vehemently asserted, that the Parish was an essentially secular Authority, of immemorial antiquity, connected with, or identical with, the Township or the Manor, we cannot pretend to decide. There is more evidence for Maitland's view that the Parish Vestry, at any rate, as an organ of secular government, was a relatively modern institution, which can hardly be carried back further than the fourteenth or fifteenth century, and that its functions as a Local Authority may have grown chiefly by the imposition upon it, by royal decree, of specific obligations and duties. However this may be, the Vestry, as the governing body of the Parish, was certainly essentially the congregation of heads of households joined together by the universal and obligatory participation in the religious service of the Church. As such, it necessarily had a communal character, irrespective of vocation; and even in its earliest historically demonstrated functions of managing 'the Parish stock', whether of money or of sheep; maintaining the fabric of the church and seeing to the upkeep of the churchyard and its wall; and providing the sacramental wine, it can be regarded only as an Association of Consumers. In the course of the next three centuries the Parish took on successively, not only the various duties placed upon it by statute, but also the provision and management of all sorts of services, which the inhabitants 'in Vestry assembled' decided that they required, and preferred to have provided at the common expense. The Church Rate, levied only on the basis of immemorial custom, became, in fact, a secular public revenue, applicable to such diverse purposes as the payment of any expenses necessarily incurred by the Parish Officers, the destruction of vermin, the repair of any parochial property and, at a later date, occasionally even the purchase of substitutes for any parishioners unfortunate enough to be drawn for service in the militia. The Parish, under the government of the inhabitants 'in Vestry assembled' (though always remaining entangled in the ecclesiastical organization, dominated by the Incumbent and the Incumbent's Churchwarden, and subject to interference by the Archdeacon and the Ordinary, not to mention also the Justices of the Peace), undoubtedly took on the character, if only gradually, and so to speak unself-consciously, of an Association of Consumers.

But the Parish Vestry, with its infinite variety of constitution and activity, is an equivocal example. At the end of the seventeenth century there emerged, in one or other form, the deliberately constructed and specifically designed Association of Consumers, for the purpose of getting carried out something recognized as a governmental function. It is significant that our earliest instance is that of a voluntary association; and that its object was the performance of the most primitive of all governmental functions, namely the protection of life and property. Thus, when in 1698 the inhabitants of the Tower Hamlets were 'much perplexed by pilfering people, picklocks, housebreakers and such ill persons', and annoyed by scenes of open profligacy, which the Justices of the Peace did nothing to repress, the inhabitants themselves set to work, as members of the local Society for the Reformation of Manners; and they were soon able to report that, 'by means of this society alone, about 2000 persons have been legally prosecuted and convicted, either as keepers of houses of bawdry and disorder, or as whores, night-walkers and the like. . . . They have also been instrumental to put down several music houses, which had degenerated into notorious nurseries of lewdness and debauchery.'[1] In the latter half of the eighteenth century, with the increase of crime and disorder due to the massing of the population in industrial districts, associations formed specifically for the prosecution of felons became widely prevalent all over England. There was, it must be remembered, no public prosecutor. It was left to any aggrieved persons to incur the trouble of getting a thief arrested and committed to prison, and then the expense and labour of preferring an indictment, producing witnesses and engaging counsel. The result was that thefts and assaults were committed with impunity. The society for the prosecution of felons undertook the task for any of its members, and sometimes maintained its own paid officials, who were sworn in as Constables to apprehend offenders. Thus, the farmers of the village of Diss, in Norfolk, formed, in 1777, their own association for apprehending and prosecuting horse-stealers. The manufacturers in the Northern industrial centres resorted to the same device, sometimes against robbers of their bleaching grounds, sometimes against the weavers to whom they gave out work, but always including in their aim the receivers of the stolen goods. Even 'the qualified sportsmen of England', we read, 'associate in clubs for the better detection of those who are prohibited from killing, or

[1] *An Account of the Rise and Progress of the Religious Societies in the City of London, etc., and of the Endeavours for Reformation of Manners which have been made therein,* by Josiah Woodward, 1698, pp. 74, 78, 79.

having game in their possession, many of whom, it must be confessed, have been prosecuted with a resentful warmth which the nature of the offence did not seem fully to justify'.[1] The most usual of these police associations was, however, that of the property owners of a given Parish or district. The Manchester newspaper of 1772 repeatedly advertises the existence of a society 'for the more effectual security of this town, the neighbouring towns and the country adjacent, against house-breaking, thieves, and receivers of stolen goods', by means of the prompt prosecution of depredators on the property of the subscribers. In 1784 'several robberies and burglaries having been lately committed in the Parish and village of Twickenham, the nobility, gentry and other inhabitants have entered into a subscription for the apprehending and prosecuting to the utmost any person who shall be guilty of any robbery or felony in the said Parish'.[2] As late as 1811–12 there is a renewed outburst of these associations, largely connected, we imagine, with the Luddite outrages; and in 1819 they again abound, perhaps even to a greater extent than at any previous period. In 1827 it is reported that 'associations against thieves have been formed in all the districts of the country'.[3] They continue throughout the first half of the nineteenth century, principally in the rural districts; and they do not entirely disappear until the universal establishment of the County Constabulary after 1856.

[1] *Hints respecting the Public Police*, by Rev. H. Zouch, J.P., 1786, p. 3.

[2] *Gazetteer*, 19 January 1784.

[3] *The Subordinate Magistracy and Parish System considered*, by Rev. C. D. Brereton (Norwich, 1827), p. 9.

It was, however, naturally in connexion with the new constructive services rendered necessary by the Industrial Revolution that witnessed the greatest development of these Associations of Consumers for the performance of governmental functions. Local Authorities were organized for the construction and improvement of harbours. Others, like that of the Manchester traders in 1776, dealt with the erection of market buildings, and the daily administration of the markets in the growing trading centres. The Turnpike Trusts, which eventually reconstructed, at the instance, and largely at the cost of the principal local users, all the main roads, constituted the most numerous class; and they drew their considerable revenue from the very persons who enjoyed the conveniences that they supplied. But the greatest development, as we have described in detail, was in the organization of the services required by the multiplication of houses and the ever-increasing traffic of the town streets. The watching, lighting, paving, cleansing and otherwise improving the rapidly increasing urban aggregations became the most imperative of the tasks of Local Government. In nearly all cases these urban services began in voluntary associations of the principal inhabitants. Sometimes the association was transient only, and merely voluntary, as when the leading parishioners of the little town of Ashford in Kent subscribed, once for all, the necessary sum to pave the principal streets. More frequently, the association was that of the owners and occupiers of a district—in some cases those of a particular 'square' in a Metropolitan Parish—who joined together to provide the lamps or the watchmen, the pavement or the sweeping necessary for their own comfort. In such cases what invariably happened was that the voluntary basis was presently found to be inadequate or inconvenient; and the association obtained a Local Act compelling all the inhabitants to pay their shares of the annual expenses. We have sufficiently described in this volume the great development of Local Authorities established under their own Local Acts, which, between 1748 and 1836, gradually came to be, so far as specifically 'municipal' administration was concerned, the most important form of English Local Government. What impresses the student of their records is the complete contrast, alike in conception and in constitutional structure, between these characteristic Local Authorities of 1748–1836, and the earlier Manorial Courts and Municipal Corporations that they succeeded. The Paving, Lighting, Police or Improvement Trustees or Commissioners were, in fact, the representatives of Associations of Consumers, in which membership was locally obligatory.

It was characteristic of this new form of governmental organization that it had absolutely no connexion with, and, indeed, practically no consciousness of, the producers of the commodities and services which it supplied. When each inhabitant was under obligation to supply and light the lantern at his door, to pave and sweep the street in front of his own house or workshop; to supply his own horses or his own labour for the mending of the roads he used; to maintain at his cost the bit of primitive embankment that protected his holding from the flood, or even to perform in his turn the duties of the various Parish offices, it was of his own pains and costs, his own efforts and sacrifices in the process of production that he was most vividly conscious. But the minutes of the Manchester Police Commissioners or the Westminster Paving Commissioners exhibit these representatives of the consumers organizing their growing services, and giving out their extensive contracts, on the basis of buying labour as a commodity, just like lamp irons or paving-stone; quite unconscious, indeed, that it is sentient beings whom they are enlisting, and the conditions of human lives that they are determining. All that they were concerned with—and this, in their inexperience of public administration, they lamentably failed to secure—was 'buying in the cheapest market', and getting the work done at the lowest possible monetary cost to the constituency that they taxed. Among the crowds of nondescript unskilled workers who were concerned in work of this character there was, at that time, no Trade Unionism, or protective combination of any kind. Taken in conjunction with the rapidly spreading Benthamite philosophy the result was the rooting of the growing municipal services, so far as concerned the great bulk of the manual labourers by whom these services were performed, in a morass of 'sweating', out of which it did not emerge until the last decades of the nineteenth century.

But whilst the organization of public services by the representatives of the Associations of Consumers that we have described took on, so far as the conditions of the wage-earners were concerned, all the characteristics of the capitalist employment that it quite frankly imitated, the fact must not be ignored that this collective or communal organization contained within it the germ of an actual supersession or capitalist enterprise —a supersession not in the interest of the producers of the services but in that of the whole body of consumers. For the most part the services organized by the new Local Authorities were not those in which the private capitalist had hitherto found a source of profit. The maintenance of the highways, the paving of the town streets, the watching, cleansing and lighting of the thoroughfares, and the provision of sewers by the new Local Authorities deprived no private capitalist of his business; and even increased his opportunities for profit-making as a contractor for the necessary works. And though here and there a Lord of the Manor or a fortunate landowner found himself in possession of a profitable market or bridge, a ferry or even a harbour as part of his estate, the provision of similar conveniences elsewhere did not seem to threaten any encroachment on private enterprise. In the nineteenth century, however, there arose, among some of the new Local Authorities claims and aspirations to serve the public of consumers in ways which purported to dispense with the toll of private profit. We have described how the Manchester Police Commissioners in 1809 fought unsuccessfully in favour of a public provision of the water supply, in opposition to a capitalist company, avowedly on the ground that 'it would be contrary to sound policy to entrust the furnishing and control of this important article of food and cleanliness, on which the health and comfort of the inhabitants depend, to persons whose sole object will be the promotion of their own private interest, and who are induced to the undertaking from no other motive'.[1] Parliament, on that occasion, gave the victory to the capitalist company; but the Association of Consumers, which the Manchester citizens had secured in their statutory Police Commissioners, was already beginning a more significant enterprise. Whilst capitalist promoters in other towns were projecting profit-making gas companies, the Manchester Police Commissioners, from 1807 onwards, were making gas by a municipal staff, in municipal retorts, for municipal use, and supplying this new means of lighting to all the inhabitants who desired it. For no less than seventeen years this municipal enterprise was conducted without statutory authority, this being obtained only in 1824; and then less from any deliberate act of policy by Parliament than by a happy accident. This incipient Municipal Socialism did not fail to be denounced by those who objected to interference with capitalist enterprise; but it proved to be the beginning, in all parts of the country, of an increasing volume and range of 'municipal trading', often in actual supersession of capitalist profit-making, the whole scope of which it is impossible, at the present day, even to forecast.[2]

The reader will now appreciate how this new form of Local Government by Associations of Consumers, empirically evolved in the course of the eighteenth century, acted and reacted on the contemporary movement towards Political Democracy. In every act of

[1] *History of the Origin and Progress of the Water-Supply in Manchester*, 1851.

[2] See the authors' *Constitution for the Socialist Commonwealth of Great Britain*, 1920.

their administration, all these various bodies representing the mass of undifferentiated citizens of particular areas, necessarily had forced on their attention the fact that the producers of each commodity or service constituted only a tiny minority, whilst the consumers, for whom the commodity was produced or the service performed, were the whole of the inhabitants. When the Westminster Paving Commissioners hired gangs of labourers to put down the Aberdeen granite and York sandstone on which the surging traffic walked or drove in comfort, it was obvious that the few score labourers were serving hundreds of thousands of citizens, rich and poor, men, women and children. The dozen or two of workmen whom the Manchester Police Commissioners hired to make gas to light the whole town were plainly serving the whole of the inhabitants. The Benthamite formula of seeking the greatest good of the greatest number seemed to imply a complete subordination of the interests of the municipal employees to those of the ratepaying citizens. At the same time, the current Radical conception of the 'Rights of Man', and the necessary union of taxation with representation, irresistibly led towards a consumers' or ratepayers' Democracy. For nearly the whole of the nineteenth century the only question agitating the successive generations of 'reformers' seemed to be how exactly this exclusively territorial Democracy was to be organized.

Government by Elected Representatives

The conception of government by representatives of the whole community was, as we have shown, not embodied in the local institutions of the eighteenth century. The distinctly oligarchical expedient of a Close Body recruiting itself by co-option was the dominant, if not the universal, device of all the constitutions resting on the decaying remnants of vocational organization. The right of the persons charged with carrying out any service to nominate their colleagues and successors, was taken for granted in the essentially vocational organizations of the seventeenth and eighteenth centuries. The new Statutory Authorities for Special Purposes frequently adopted a similar oligarchical principle in their various forms of Co-option. Among the Local Authorities of this period the meeting of inhabitants in Vestry assembled was the only one in which can be discerned a communal Democracy. But this nascent Democracy had not then developed a representative system. It was, indeed, not without reluctance and many complaints,[1] that Englishmen abandoned the simpler expedient of government by the common consent of all those concerned. At the end of the eighteenth century it was this common agreement of the inhabitants, by tradition and practice *the principal inhabitants*, rather than decision by a numerical majority, whether of representatives or ratepayers, for which, particularly in matters of Local Government, men yearned. And

[1] 'One of the great books that remain to be written', we are told by F. W. Maitland, 'is the History of the Majority. Our habit of treating the voice of a majority as equivalent to the voice of an all is so deeply engrained that we hardly think that it has a history. But a history it has, and there is fiction there: not fiction if that term implies falsehood or caprice, but a slow extension of old words and old thoughts beyond the old facts.

down to the end of the eighteenth century, this note of common agreement, as the end of discussion and debate, remained strong. 'It is most convenient', says a widely read eighteenth-century law-book, 'that every Parish Act', done at a Vestry 'be entered in the Parish book of accounts,'—not, be it noted, as having been carried by a majority vote, but with 'every man's hand consenting to it . . . set thereto; for then it will be a certain rule for the Churchwardens to go by.'[1] 'Agreed and consented to by us whose names . . . are hereunto subscribed' is, in fact a phrase constantly found preceding the lists of signatures by which the inhabitants in Vestry were accustomed to authenticate their minutes.

What broke down this old conception of government by consent of all the persons concerned was the surging into the Vestry meetings of such populous Parishes as Manchester or Leeds, Woolwich or St. Pancras, of large numbers of parishioners, who were naturally for the most part, not the 'principal inhabitants' to whom the government had habitually been left, and whose turbulent proceedings led to the withdrawal from attendance of the quieter and 'more respectable' inhabitants. In a few Parishes the practical impossibility of 'government by public meeting' of this sort led to the establishment, quite extra-legally, of a Parish Committee, elected at a Vestry meeting, which took upon itself the whole functions of Parish government, merely reporting to and seeking covering sanction from Open Vestry meetings held at periodical intervals.

[1] Shaw's *Parish Law*, p. 55; *The Parish and the County*, p. 52.

We have described the highly organized and remarkably efficient government of the great Parish of Liverpool by such an extra-legal committee.[1]

But such a Parish Committee had in it the weakness of possessing no legal authority. The Parish Officers could, at any moment, decline to act upon its resolutions. Any recalcitrant ratepayer might invoke the interference of the Justices of the Peace or the Courts of Law against its action. Such Parish Committees were, in fact, upset in various Parishes.[2] An alternative expedient, and one that could be employed also to strengthen a Parish Committee, was to take a poll, in order to ascertain the real opinion of the whole mass of parishioners, who (contrary to the opinion of some legal authorities) were allowed to vote whether or not they had been present at the meeting at which the poll was demanded. In adopting the device of a poll of all the parishioners, the Vestry, it will be seen, was abandoning the conception of government by common consent, in favour of government by the decision of the majority for the time being. In 1819, the well-known Sturges Bourne Act enabled any Parish to appoint annually in Open Vestry a Committee empowered to carry out, not, indeed, all the work of the Parish, but all matters relating to the relief of the poor, and reporting to meetings of the Open Vestry at least twice a year. So far the Act was 'adoptive' only. But the statute also provided that, in all Parishes outside the City of London and Southwark, and not governed by

[1] *The Parish and the County*, pp. 134–45.

[2] In St. Giles, Cripplegate 1731; and in St. Mary Abbots, Kensington, in 1776; see *The Parish and the County*, p. 143.

Local Acts of their own, the ratepayers should each have from one to six votes, in proportion to the rateable value of their premises. It was not foreseen that the recording of these various votes necessarily involved taking separately the decision of each voter, and thus a poll which could not, in practice, be confined to those persons who had been present at the previous Vestry meeting. Thus Sturges Bourne's Act introduced, in effect, into English Local Government, at the option of any one ratepayer in attendance at the meeting, a popular Referendum upon any decision whatsoever. We have described how this limitation of the work of the Parish Committee to the one function of poor relief, coupled with the introduction of an obligatory Referendum, heavily weighted in favour of the larger ratepayers, created confusion and disorder in the Vestries of the larger Parishes. Any section outvoted at the meeting immediately claimed a poll of the Parish; and this had to be granted as a matter of legal right. As the wealthier classes abstained from the public meeting, and, moreover, had most to gain by the strict counting of the plural votes, it was usually the Tories who demanded this Referendum, and the Radicals who objected to it. This unpremeditated experiment in the use of the Referendum—handicapped as it was by every unfavourable circumstance—practically introduced a fatal element of discord into the most smoothly working constitutions of populous parishes. Even at Liverpool, where Toryism and the Church of England dominated the working men as well as the upper classes, we see, from 1828 onward, a constantly increasing number of appeals from the

Vestry meeting to the poll. In one year (1832) no fewer than eight of these polls were taken, on such questions as the amount of salary to be paid to an official, the election of Churchwardens and Sidesmen, the assessment of the owners of cottage property, and whether the Churchwardens' account should or should not be passed. The active spirits who, in the heated years of the Reform controversy, carried the Open Vestry meetings, were habitually defeated at the poll. They revenged themselves on the Tory party by turning the half-yearly meeting at the old Parish Church into a pandemonium. At Leeds, if the Non-conformist Radicals carried the election of Churchwardens at one of the large and turbulent Vestry meetings that we have described, the Tories insisted on a poll of the Parish. From 1833 onwards this becomes a regular practice. When a poll was refused, they obtained a mandamus ordering it to be conceded. The Tory newspaper, in April 1835, candidly avowed, that 'the only method now left to the friends of law and order is to appeal from such packed Vestries to the Parish at large. Nor will the appeal be in vain. . . . Rated females are entitled to vote as well as males. We do not wish for a gynocracy; but we are sufficiently gallant to perceive that too many of the wayward lords of creation are disposed to make a bad world of it; therefore the sooner the ladies interfere the better.'[1]

The first embodiment in legislation of this change of opinion was 'An Act for the Better Regulation of Vestries and for the Appointment of Auditors of

[1] *Leeds Intelligencer*, 25 April 1835; *The Parish and the County*, pp. 168–9.

Accounts in Certain Parishes of England and Wales'.[1] Whilst Sturges Bourne in 1818–19 had merely sought to regularize and supplement the decision and control of the open Vestry Meeting, another aristocratic reformer, John Cam Hobhouse, more under the Benthamite influence, a dozen years later, gave to every Parish the opportunity of superseding the Vestry altogether by a body of elected representatives in whom the whole government of the Parish was vested. Based on ratepayers' suffrage, equal voting, the ballot and annual elections, with provisions for publicity and an independent audit, 'Hobhouse's Act', as it was universally called, was 'the first legislative attempt to apply the principle of municipal self-government to the inorganic masses of population and property forming the modern additions to London'. But the Act applied only to those Parishes in which the ratepayers chose to adopt it on a poll; and its operation was, in fact, confined to a relatively few large Parishes, principally those having Select Vestries in the Metropolitan area.

Government by bodies of elected representatives was, however, by this time definitely accepted as the necessary form for new constitutions. For some years it had been becoming steadily more usual in Improvement Commissions. The Manchester Police Commissioners, at that time perhaps the most important Local Authority—apart from the exceptionally busy Municipal Corporations of Liverpool and Bristol—outside the City of London, were changed, by the 1828 Act, from being a class of all the substantial

[1] 1 & 2 William IV, c. 60.

householders, thousands in number, to an elected assembly of 240 members. When the time came for the urgently needed reform of the Poor Law, in the first flush of triumph of the Reformed Parliament, though much was said against the new principles on which relief was to be given, and against both the Union area and the workhouse, not a voice was raised in opposition to the work being entrusted, not to the ratepayers at large, but to a representative body.[1]

The seal was set upon the principle of government by a representative body by the agitation for the reform of the Municipal Corporations, which culminated in the Municipal Corporations Act of 1835. The public resentment of the Close Bodies which had continued to govern the property and privileges of the Boroughs was doubtless mainly political in its origin. So far as Local Government was concerned, the complaint was not so much that the Corporations performed the Municipal functions badly, as that they did not, in the great majority of cases, perform them at all. The Reformed Parliament of 1833 willingly saw the appointment of a Royal Commission to inquire into the Municipal Corporations; and the habit of the time of manning all such Commissions by eager young intellectuals of Whig opinions determined, as we have shown, the

[1] So strong was the tendency towards entrusting Local Government to representative bodies that the very existence of another alternative was ignored. It is usually forgotten that the report of the Poor Law Inquiry Commissioners of 1832 was as adverse to the administration of elected Parish Committees, Select Vestries under Sturges Bourne's Act, and Local Act Incorporations of Guardians of the Poor as it was to that of Open Vestries and the compulsorily serving Parish Officers.

tenor of the verdict.[1] There was, in fact, at the moment, no rival, among those with reforming instincts, to the Benthamite political philosophy which had erected representative Democracy, based on universal suffrage and ballot voting, into a panacea. The Municipal Corporation Commissioners (with a dissenting minority of two only) made their recommendations with no uncertain voice. Lord Melbourne's Cabinet, pressed for time, found no other policy. Public opinion throughout the country gave the reform overwhelming support. The House of Commons put up practically no opposition; and even Sir Robert Peel could see no alternative. Only in the House of Lords was the principle of representative Democracy seriously contested; and here, as we have described, the opposition was eventually driven to give way, owing to the refusal of the Tory leaders in the House of Commons to support the Upper House. The passing of the Municipal Corporations Act in 1835, even subject to the concessions that were, by way of compromise, made to the House of Lords, meant, for English Local Government, much more than the substitution, in 178 towns, of an elected Town Council for the former Close Body. Coupled with the unopposed adoption in the Poor Law Amendment Act of 1834 of a representative body for the administration of the Poor Law, it meant, as the subsequent history has demonstrated, the definite acceptance of representative Democracy throughout the whole sphere of Local Government. Francis Place was right in 1836 when he foresaw, as the outcome of Lord Melbourne's Act, 'the whole country'

[1] *The Manor and the Borough*, pp. 740–51.

becoming eventually 'Municipalized'; by which he meant, 'an incorporation of the whole country which will be the basis of a purely representative government'.[1]

It is worth notice how sweeping, in many respects, was the revolution thus made, and how little public attention its universality attracted at the time. With the one significant exception of the red thread of Property Qualification running through all forms of authority, which was retained intact, and in some ways even strengthened by the Reformed House of Commons, the barriers which had divded the English people into mutually exclusive groups were, in 1834–6, so far as Local Government was concerned, almost wholly broken down. In the government of his Parish, his Poor Law Union and his Borough, the undifferentiated citizen-consumer, electing whatever representatives he chose became, in effect, supreme. The vocational qualification, once the very basis of Manor and Borough, finds no place in the reorganized municipality.[2] Less complete, but scarcely less significant, was the

[1] Place to Parkes, 3 January 1836, Add. MSS. 35, 150, p. 102; *The Manor and the Borough*, p. 751.

[2] The reservation (by the Municipal Corporations Act, 1835, sec. 2) to the existing Freemen, their wives, children and apprentices, of all rights of property and beneficial exemptions that they enjoyed in 1835, including the right to vote for Members of Parliament, was but a transient exception. It may be added that the Municipal Corporations omitted from the Act retained their old constitutions, to be swept away (with the exception of that of the City of London) only in 1883. The nominally vocational basis of the Liverymen of the City of London, with their equally nominal participation in the election of the Lord Mayor and a few other officers, remains, we believe, in 1922, the only survival of the old vocational organization in English Local Government.

tacit abandonment, so far as concerned the government of the Parish, the new Poor Law Union and the urban area under Improvement Commissioners, of the barrier of sex. Women occupiers had never been declared to be ineligible for the onerous Parish offices, any more than for those of the ancient organizations for maintaining the embankments and sluices of districts within the jurisdiction of Courts of Sewers; and they had never been excluded from attendance and voting at the Open Vestries. Now, under both Sturges Bourne's and Hobhouse's Acts, the rights of occupiers in the government of the Parish were definitely made independent of sex; and this precedent was followed in the Poor Law Amendment Act of 1834, as well as in the General Highways Act of 1835, not merely in respect of the right to elect the members of the Board of Guardians and Highway Boards, but also, as it seems, in respect of eligibility for election.[1] But the Municipal Corporations Act, 1835, failed to go so far. Though the status of Burges was extended to inhabitant 'occupiers',[2] they were, until 1869, definitely required to be males.

[1] It remained uncertain, however, whether a married woman could either vote or be elected; not because of any disability by sex, but because it was doubtful whether a woman 'under coverture', being (until the Married Women's Property Act of 1870) unable legally to own property, could legally, in her own person, be an 'occupier'. The point can hardly be said to have been definitely and generally decided in her favour until the passing of the Sex Disqualification Removal Act of 1920.

[2] Having been occupiers within the Borough for two whole years, inhabitant householders therein or within seven miles, British subjects, not defaulters in payment of rates, and not receiving parochial relief or corporate charities within twelve months past.

The most important enfranchisement, however, was that gained by the sweeping away of religious exclusiveness. Owing to the curious heedlessness which Parliament and the Government displayed about the Parish, neither Nonconformists nor, as it seems, Roman Catholics, were ever legally disqualified, either for membership of the Open Vestry, or from service in the Parish offices, any more than from membership of the Juries of the Manor or of the Court of Sewers, or of the offices connected therewith. They were, however, normally excluded from all Close Bodies, whether Select Vestries or Municipal Corporations, as they were from the Commission of the Peace, and from the County shrievalty. The Statutory Authorities for Special Purposes, growing up in the course of the eighteenth century, had entirely ignored differences of religion; and the reorganization of Parish government by Sturges Bourne's and Hobhouse's Acts, together with the Poor Law Amendment Act itself, tacitly adopted the same policy. Most potent of all, however, was the like sweeping away of religious disabilities in the reformed Boroughs by the Municipal Corporations Act, which brought to a summary end a much-prized monopoly of the Established Church. This part of 'Corporation reform' it was that its author, Lord Melbourne, regarded as the most revolutionary. 'You may not', he felt, 'see all the consequences of this tormorrow; but you have given by law a permanent power in all the centres of industry and intelligence to the Dissenters which they never had before, and which they never could have had otherwise. They are the classes who will really gain by the change, not the mob or the theorists; every year their strength will be felt more and more at elections and their influence in legislation. Depend upon it, it is the Established Church, not the hereditary peerage, that has need to set its house in order.'[1]

The Salaried Officer

The student will have realized how universally prevalent, down to the latter part of the seventeenth century, was the conception of the performance of all the work of Local Government by unpaid, compulsorily serving and constantly changing average citizens. For many offices, however, notably those which could be made remunerative to the holder by the exaction of sufficient fees, the alternative principle of freehold tenure was adopted. Both these conceptions yielded during the eighteenth century, but only slowly and incompletely, to a fundamentally different principle of administration. The change was threefold. In place of the constantly changing service of ordinary citizens, there is the continuous employment of the same person, who necessarily developed a certain professional expertness. Instead of the independent authority enjoyed by the unpaid citizen who was appointed to exercise as he thought best the customary or statutory powers of the Churchwarden, the Overseer, the Constable or the Surveyor of Highways, or the absolute autonomy of the holders of such freehold offices as Clerk of the Peace or Coroner, there is the employment of a salaried agent to carry out, as he was bid, the

[1] *Memoirs of Lord Melbourne*, by W. T. McCullagh Torrens, 1878, vol. ii, p. 156; *The Manor and the Borough*, p. 750.

orders of the superior Authority. Finally there emerges, at the very end of the period, in contradistinction to the notion that any man of honesty and zeal is equal to the duties of any office whatsoever, the modern conception of specialist qualifications, without which even the most virtuous candidate could not be deemed fit for appointment.

It is needless to enumerate all the instances of this change of principle. One of the earliest examples was the gradual and silent passing away of the immemorial freehold office of Parish Clerk. From the latter part of the seventeenth century onward, we find, especially in the South of England, vacancies being filled, here and there, by the appointment of a Vestry Clerk, whose office was regulated neither by custom nor by statute; who was paid such salary as the Vestry chose, and who could be required to act in any way the Vestry desired.[1] An even greater innovation, and one long characteristic chiefly of Northern and Midland Parishes, was the appointment of a 'standing', 'perpetual' or 'hireling' Overseer, to whom a salary was assigned, and on whom the whole onerous duty of the Overseer was cast, to be carried out under the direction of the Churchwardens, the Parish Committee, or the inhabitants in Vestry Assembled. In 1819 this institution of a salaried Overseer was legalized by Sturges Bourne's Act, when it was very widely adopted.[2] When the

[1] A humbler servant of the Vestry, scarcely earlier in origin than the Vestry Clerk, was the Parish Beadle, who could be used for any service whatsoever, and whose duties during the eighteenth century became steadily more multifarious.

[2] In some urban Parishes paid watchmen supplemented the efforts of the unpaid Constable, or replaced him.

Parish established a workhouse, it frequently, as we have seen, put the management out to contract. But otherwise it had to appoint a paid 'master' or 'governor' of the institution, frequently other servants, and occasionally even a surgeon and a chaplain. Only in a few cases do we find a salaried Surveyor of Highways. But at the beginning of the nineteenth century, some of the principal roads were coming to be reconstructed by the promoted stone mason, Telford, one of the founders of the Institute of Civil Engineers, the premier professional organization of the most scientific of modern professions. Owing to his influence a clause was inserted in the Act of 1818 (merging into one five Turnpike Trusts concerned with a portion of the Holyhead road) compelling the new body to employ a professional civil engineer as their surveyor for the whole of their mileage of road. In other parts of the country the management of the Turnpike Trusts came, more and more, as we have already described, to be undertaken by Macadam and his son. 'Gratuitous services', Macadam urged, 'are ever temporary and local; they are dependent on the residence and life of the party; and have always disappointed expectation. Skill and executive labour must be adequately paid for, if expected to be constantly and usefully exerted; and, if so exerted, the price is no consideration when compared with the advantage to the public.'[1] Equally scientific was Macadam's organization of his constantly increasing staff of subordinate road engineers, representing the coming in of the definite professional qualifications. The same tendency is to be seen in the

[1] *The Story of the King's Highway*, p. 173.

whole experience of the Improvement Commissioners. For the new duties and new services, in so far as these were not put out to contract, salaried officers were employed. These gradually became professionally expert gas engineers or gas managers, police superintendents, managers of markets, harbourmasters, or what we now call Municipal Surveyors or Municipal Engineers. And although the County Justices continued, right down to our own day, to be advised by such independent freeholders as the Clerk of the Peace and the Coroner, in one County after another they appointed salaried officers to manage the repairs and rebuilding of the bridges (for which the Shropshire Justices were wise enough to engage Telford), and, eventually, in the nineteenth century, even salaried governors of the new prisons in substitution for the old-time gaoler who lived by his fees and other exactions. Not the least important of these substitutions, though one long confined to the Metropolis and only extended to a few provincial towns, was that of stipendiary magistrates for the unpaid Justices, who had too often proved themselves to be 'Trading Justices'. These Metropolitan stipendiaries, at first secretly developing from what we have called the Court Justice, and statutorily authorized only in 1792, were, in the nineteenth century, always appointed from the Bar, and were thus always professionally qualified for the office.[1] Finally, the Poor Law Amendment Act of

[1] It is interesting to find the notorious younger Mainwaring in 1821, a few months before his discreditable career as unpaid Justice of the Peace and Treasurer of the County of Middlesex was brought to an end, unctuously expounding the superiority of the 'Great Unpaid', (*Observations on the Police*

1834 and the Municipal Corporations Act of 1835 definitely adopted the principle of the execution of the work of Local Government by salaried officers, appointed by the Local Authority, subject to its orders, and holding office only at its will. What was absolutely unknown as an instrument of Local Government in the seventeenth century—a hierarchical bureaucracy working under a body of elected representatives—became in the nineteenth century, not only the succesor of the holders of freehold offices and the unpaid, compulsorily serving citizens, but also, in one service after another, a practicable alternative to the profit-making contractor or capitalist entrepreneur.[1]

The Innovations of Statute Law

It is difficult to realize, in the twentieth century, how dominant in the whole range of Local Government was still, in the seventeenth century, the Local Custom and the Common Law. At the beginning of that century

of the Metropolis, by G. B. Mainwaring, 1821, pp. 128–9, 133; *The Parish and the County*, pp. 565, 579–80).

' "To lay down the principle that men are to serve for nothing", said Cobbett, in criticizing the system of unpaid magistrates, "puts me in mind of the servant who went on hire, who, being asked what wages he demanded, said he wanted no wages: for that he always found about the house little things to pick up" ' (*The Village Labourer*, by J. L. and B. Hammond, 1911).

[1] It was this introduction of the salaried official as the alternative to the unpaid, compulsorily serving citizen, taking his turn in public office, that Toulmin Smith denounced as 'one of the most alarming symptoms of the successful attempts that have, of late years, been made—under cover, at the best, of a pedantic doctrinairism—to overlay the free Institutions of England, their working and their spirit alike, by the system of Bureaucracy and Functionarism' (*The Parish, its Powers and Obligations at Law*, 1857, by Toulmin Smith, p. 211).

no less an authority than Chief Justice Coke could be quoted in support of the inviolable supremacy of the Common Law, and in depreciation of the innovating statutes by which Parliament was beginning spasmodically to interfere with it.[1] A couple of centuries later, Toulmin Smith passionately clung to the idea that English 'Local Self-Government', a glorious heritage from 'time out of mind', was independent of Parliament, inviolable by innovating statutes, and inherently superior in moral, if not also in legal authority, to Parliament itself.[2] Prior to 1689, indeed, the innovations of Parliament in Local Government had been few and far between, and more by way of prescribing new functions than in materially altering either the constitution of Manor or Parish, Borough or County, or their ancient authority. But at the close of the seventeenth and throughout the eighteenth century we find, as we have described, ever-increasing crowds of innovating statutes. To the hundreds of brand-new Local Authorities that they set up, we have had to devote a whole volume. As the century wore to its close, Act after Act, of a character once unusual, imposed general rules and wide-reaching prohibitions upon all the Parishes in respect of their relief of the poor, upon all the Turnpike Trusts in their

[1] 'It is not almost credible to foresee, when any maxim or fundamental law of this realm, is altered, what dangerous inconveniencies do follow. . . . New things which have fair pretences are most commonly hurtful to the Commonwealth; for commonly they tend to the hurt and oppression of the subject, and not to that glorious end that at first was pretended' (Coke, 4 Inst. 41).

[2] See, for instance, *Local Self-Government and Centralization*, by J. Toulmin Smith, 1851, p. 23.

maintenance of the roads, upon all the Courts of Quarter Sessions in their upkeep of the bridges and their management of the Houses of Correction and County gaols. But it was in the nineteenth century, and particularly in its second, third and fourth decades, that this tendency for Parliament to prescribe, by statute, general rules in supersession of Local Custom and the Common Law for all the Local Authorities from one end of England to the other, became a regular habit. Sir Samuel Romilly induced the House of Commons summarily to cut down the oppressive powers of all the bodies of Incorporated Guardians under Local Acts; by Sturges Bourne's Act and Hobhouse's Act, all the Parishes were reformed; nearly every year saw a new General Turnpike Act; the lunatic asylums, the prisons, the roads, the relief of the poor, were made the subject of statutes which applied to every Local Authority dealing with these functions of Local Government. What had empirically become the practice of the House of Commons was raised by the Benthamite philosophy almost to a dogma. Parliament became increasingly careless of local peculiarities and local customs, and more and more disposed empirically to supersede them by a national uniformity based on the current social philosophy. To those who were directly or indirectly inspired by Bentham and James Mill, this national uniformity in what was judged rationally to be the utilitarian course seemed, in the new statecraft, merely obvious wisdom. Thus, the way was open for the Reformed Parliament in a couple of sessions to smooth out of existence, by two all-embracing statutes, the infinite variety of Local Customs and particular

Charters or By-laws that had continued to characterize the Municipal Corporation, and all the casual habits and peculiarities which had marked the separate administration, by more than a hundred incorporated bodies of Guardians and over ten thousand autonomous Parishes and Townships, of the Elizabethan Poor Law.

The Rise of Specialized Central Departments

The gradual development of general statute law, introducing a measure of uniformity in the several branches of Local Government, was accompanied by a still more gradual and tentative development of the authority of the National Executive, with regard to one function after another; taking eventually the form of the establishment of specialized Government Departments of supervision and control.

We may begin with the service of the prevention and punishment of crime and disorder, in which the intervention of the Government long manifested itself, not so much in a regulation and control of Local Authorities, as in a direct utilization of the Lord-Lieutenant and the Justices of the Peace as agents of a centralized National Executive. During the whole of the eighteenth century, down to the French Revolution at any rate, this intervention came to little more than the issue of periodical proclamations, sometimes merely on the accession of a new sovereign, sometimes on the occurrence of some riot or tumult, commanding 'all our Judges, Mayors, Sheriffs, Justices of the Peace, and all other of our officers and ministers, both ecclesiastical and civil, to be very vigilant and strict in the discovery and effectual prosecution and punishment of all offenders'. But although these proclamations were solemnly read at the Assizes, circulated to the Lord-Lieutenants and printed in the *London Gazette*, no one, in ordinary times, took much notice of them, and no attempt was made by the Government, either by calling for specific reports or by further investigation, to make the solemn formality effective. Nor were the other Privy Council proclamations of the eighteenth century of much more interest to the student of Local Government. From time to time some particularly heinous murder or street robbery, some exceptional deer stealing or forest depredations, would provoke a verbose proclamation, of which the only operative part would be the offer of a large reward, often £100, for the discovery and conviction of the culprits.[1]

After the outbreak of the French Revolution—still more after the Peace of 1815—the attitude of the National Executive changes. There is no more effective action than before against mere licentiousness or ordinary crime. But, at any rate from 1815 onward, the Ministers strove with might and main to put down the pupular tumults and mob disorders, which, with some justification, they now associated with incipient rebellion. This methodical repression is revealed in the reports and doings of the Government spies and informers, which so much impressed the members of

[1] See, for instance, the proclamations against street robberies and murders of 21 January 1720, 29 February 1727, 9 July 1735, 7 November 1744, 11 January 1749 and 20 December 1750; those of 2 February and 8 October 1723 against deer stealers; and that of 12 June 1728 against the 'great destruction . . . in the Forest of Needwood' (MS. Acts of Privy Council, George I and George II).

the Privy Council and of the various Secret Committees of both Houses of Parliament; in the constant instructions which were given to the Justices of the Peace acting in the disturbed districts, and in the activities of the 'Bow Street runners', in co-operation with such willing agents as Nadin, the permanent police officer of the Boroughreeve and Constables of Manchester. Even more repressive and alarming to the ordinary citizen was the readiness with which, in 1795–1800, in 1811–12, between 1816 and 1819, and in the rural counties of the South of England in 1830–31, the Government made use of the military forces, horse, foot and artillery, in disorders often connected only with industrial disputes, which, at the present day, would be quite successfully dealt with by the constabulary of the Local Authorities.[1]

Out of this spasmodic and so to speak revolutionary extension into the provinces of the authority of the National Executive, there developed, to some extent under Lord Sidmouth between 1816 and 1822, and more systematically under Sir Robert Peel between 1822 and 1830, a more continuous supervision by the Home Office than had ever before been customary, of the County Justices and the Corporate magistracies in their capacity of Police and Prison Authorities. The Home Office in 1815 got passed an Act requiring all Prison Authorities to furnish statistical reports of their gaols and Houses of Correction; and on the basis

[1] See for all this, the Home Office archives, 1795–1832, now accessible in the Public Record Office; and the able and interesting books of Mr. and Mrs. Hammond (*The Village Labourer, 1760–1832*; *The Town Labourer, 1760–1831*; and *The Skilled Labourer, 1760–1832*).

of these reports, supported by the recommendations of House of Commons Committees of 1820 and 1822, Peel was able to induce Parliament to enact the Prisons Act of 1823, 'the first measure of general prison reform to be framed and enacted on the responsibility of the National Executive'.[1] This Act, besides consolidating the whole statute law relating to prisons, for the first time made it the duty of the Local Authorities for prisons to organize their administration uniformly upon a prescribed plan, which became a statutory obligation; and peremptorily required these Local Authorities to furnish quarterly to the Home Secretary detailed reports of every branch of their prison administration. This Act, applying to all the Courts of Quarter Sessions of the Counties, to the Cities of London and Westminster, and to seventeen of the principal Municipal Corporations, was the first that dictated to Local Authorities the detailed plan on which they were to exercise a branch of their own local administration; the first that made it obligatory on them to report, quarter by quarter, how their administration was actually being conducted; and the first that definitely asserted the duty of a Central Department to maintain a continuous supervision of the action of the Local Authorities in their current administration. In 1835 a second great Prisons Act, passed on the reports which the Home Office got adopted by an exceptionally authoritative Select Committee of the House of Lords,[2]

[1] 4 George IV, c. 64; *English Prisons under Local Government*, 1922, p. 73.

[2] See the voluminous five successive reports of the House of Lords Committee on the State of the Gaols and Houses of Correction, 1835; the Act 2 & 3 William IV, c. 38; and our *English Prisons under Local Government*, 1922, pp. 111-12.

prescribed a still 'greater uniformity of practice in the government' of all the prisons in England and Wales; authorized the Home Secretary to make binding regulations from time to time on all the details of administration, and subjected all the Local Authorities, for the first time, to constant inspection of their work in this branch of Local Government, by a staff of salaried professional experts, by whose outspoken critical reports, regularly submitted to Parliament and thereby published to the world, both the National Government and public opinion were kept informed of every seeming imperfection.

In another service of the Local Authorities, that of the maintenance of the highways, the new intervention of the National Executive was almost entirely concentrated within the second and third decades of the nineteenth century; and a sudden change of circumstances prevented the development of a specialized Government Department. We have told elsewhere how, at the very beginning of the nineteenth century, the Post Office became greatly troubled at the bad state of the Holyhead road; how in 1815 the Treasury summoned up courage to ask the House of Commons to vote £20,000 for the improvement of this main artery of communication with Ireland; how the work was undertaken by a new body of ten Commissioners, three of whom were Ministers of the Crown; and how, in the course of the next fifteen years, these Commissioners of the Holyhead Road, virtually a central Government Department, spent three-quarters of a million pounds, without actually superseding the Turnpike Trusts, in order to enable Telford to construct what was deemed in 1830 the 'most perfect roadmaking that has ever been attempted in any country'. Meanwhile, what was, in effect, another central Government Department, although based on an unpaid advisory board, began to press the Local Authorities to improve their roads. The Board of Agriculture, under Sir John Sinclair, from 1810 onward brought forward J. L. Macadam, with his plan for constructing a road surface both better and cheaper than any previously in use. For a couple of decades we watch the influence of the Government, and the diligence of Macadam effecting, through the Turnpike Trustees, an almost continuous and almost universal improvement in the roads—until in 1829, the amazing success of Stephenson's locomotive engine turned everybody's attention to the coming railways; and the National Executive ceased, with dramatic suddenness, to trouble itself about a service seemingly doomed to rapid obsolescence.

A great measure of permanence was gained by the intervention of the National Executive in another branch of Local Government, that which was then thought of as the Suppression of Nuisances and is now styled Public Health. Here it was the Privy Council that suddenly brought its influence to bear on the Local Authorities. In the spring of 1831 England began to be alarmed by reports that a new and frightful epidemic disease, afterwards known as Asiatic Cholera, was advancing steadily westwards through Europe. The Privy Council, after sending two doctors to St. Petersburg to report on the disease, not only put in force all the precautionary measures of quarantine, which had been used against the Levantine plague, but also, following precedents of 1721 and 1805, established a Central Board of Health of medical and other dignitaries, which issued solemn proclamations of advice to all and sundry how to keep themselves from disease. But the Asiatic Cholera paid no attention to the futilities of the Central Board of Health; and in the autumn of 1831 it broke out in Sunderland and spread rapidly, during the ensuing twelve months, to nearly all parts of the country. In this emergency the central Board of Health was reconstituted, and by Orders in Council Local Boards of Health were appointed in a large number of towns and populous places, on which were placed the local magistrates, clergy, doctors and other 'principal inhabitants'; and which were charged to suppress nuisances, and to take any elementary measures of public sanitation that commended themselves. For all this the Parish Officers were directed to pay, and the Parish Vestry was asked to provide for by rate. When some of them demurred, an Act of Parliament was hastily passed in 1832 making this financial provision obligatory on all the Parishes for which Local Boards of Health had been set up.

These Local Boards of Health, which were eventually established in nearly all towns and populous districts of any magnitude, are interesting to the student of Local Government as affording a simple instance of an *ad hoc* body; established wherever desired, independently of Municipal Corporation or Parish Vestry; nominally by appointment from above, but practically by the self-election of some zealous citizens who volunteered their services at a public meeting or otherwise, and the co-option of others; and making what was virtually a precept on the Parish Overseers for the amount of their expenditure. These Local Boards of Health all came to an end when the cholera died away, not to be revived again until there was a renewed alarm in 1848. What is more significant is the fact that the central Government Department concerned, in this case the Privy Council, continued its interest in the health work of the Local Authorities, and thus established a claim to be the Central Health Authority, which—temporarily entrusted to its creature, the much-resented Central Board of Health in 1848–54—issued in 1871 in the Local Government Board, to be still further specialized in 1919 (at least in name) by its conversion into the Ministry of Health.[1]

For the rest of the services specially characteristic of town government—in 1835 mostly in the hands of Improvement Commissioners—no specialized Government Department was set up. By the Municipal Corporations Act, 1835, it was intended and hoped that these bodies would be led voluntarily to merge themselves and their services in the reformed Municipal Corporations; and this in fact occurred, though not without much further legislation; and it took another half century for all these separate Commissions to be absorbed. But not even Lord Melbourne dared to subject the reformed Municipal Corporations in all their work to the same systematic inspection and control as he was able to enact, for them as well as for the

[1] Bentham deserves credit for his sketch of a Ministry of Health a century before such a Ministry was established; see *Works*, vol. ix, p. 443.

County Justices, in respect of their administration of prisons. The only approach to central control in the Municipal Corporations Act of 1835, is the section making it necessary for a Corporation desiring to alienate any of the Corporate real estate first to obtain the consent of the Lords Commissioners of the Treasury—a control transferred in 1871 to the Local Government Board.

A more significant example of Benthamite centralization was the establishment, by two Acts of 1836, of the Registrar-General, who was placed in control of the new machinery for the official registration of births, deaths and marriages throughout the whole of England and Wales.

The most impressive instance of the development of the influence and authority of Parliament and the National Executive into the establishment of a specialized Government Department is afforded by the history of poor relief. Throughout the eighteenth century there had been occasional statutes enlarging or amending the powers and duties of the Local Authorities. These Authorities had been permitted from time to time to unite in larger areas, to erect and maintain workhouses; and even to exercise great authority over vagrants and other persons neglecting to earn their living. They had been, by one or other Act, alternately encouraged and restrained, in this direction or that. They had, on two occasions, even been statutorily required to render statistical returns of their proceedings, which were presented to Parliament. But throughout the whole period, their action was regarded as of strictly local concern. What the Parish

Officers chose to do, the Parish Vestry to acquiesce in and the Local Justices of the Peace not to prohibit was not made the subject of any official criticism from London. In the relief of the poor the Local Authorities were, right down to 1834, left unsupervised and uncontrolled by any Government Department. The innovation of 1834 was not preceded and led up to by any tentative interference of the National Executive. Save for occasional inquiries by Committees of the House of Commons, out of which came such constitutional reforms promoted by private members of Parliament as Sturges Bourne's Act and Hobhouse's Act, there seem to have been no official preparations for the revolutionary change of 1834. What brought it about was, of course, the enormous and continued rise in the Poor Rate, which went from one million pounds in 1700 to three million in 1800, to seven million in 1820, and remained for fifteen years near that figure. Coupled with this drain on the rental of the land and buildings, on the ownership of which the authority of the governing class rested, was the realization by a large proportion of the educated classes of the widespread demoralization that was being caused by the methods of pauperization that were employed. The prevalent opinion of the Reform Parliament was in favour of drastic reform, and the celebrated Poor Law Commission was promptly appointed. But although there had been no official preparation for an administrative revolution, the permeation of 'enlightened public opinion' by the necessary political theory had been effective. Nor was the Whig Ministry averse. In the all-important Commission, the members, the secretary and the Assistant Commissioners were alike chosen from among those who had been influenced by the Benthamite philosophy. Their investigations, their discoveries and their recommendations were all dominated by the potent contemporary doctrines of Philosophic Radicalism. They were all based on the conception of local administration, not by compulsorily serving amateurs, but by salaried officials; not as each district might choose, but according to a uniform and centrally prescribed plan; yet without complete autonomy for the executive officers, who were to be supervised by an elected body, representing the rate-payers on whom the cost was to fall; and these local representative bodies were to be controlled by a central Government Department which—continuously informed by a staff of salaried, peripatetic, expert inspectors—alone would be competent to devise and enforce a policy that would be for the greatest good of the greatest number. Eagerly accepted by the Whig Ministry and the House of Commons, this drastic reform of the Poor Law was embodied in the Poor Law Amendment Act of 1834, which established, in what were called 'the three Bashaws of Somerset House', the first Government Department deliberately created exclusively for the purpose of controlling and directing Local Authorities in the execution of their work. The reader will not need to be reminded how the Poor Law Commissioners, denounced and derided, nevertheless held their own, and were continued in 1848 as the Poor Law Board; and how in 1871 this body was combined with the Public Health Department of the Privy Council and the Local Act Branch of the Home Office to become, in the Local Government Board, more explicitly than ever, the central Government Department to the authority of which all local governing bodies were subjected; and how, in 1919, the Local Government Board, following the tendency towards the specialization of Government Departments according to function, was united with the National Health Insurance Commission to constitute the Ministry of Health.

The Property Qualification

Of all the old principles of English Local Government that we described in the last chapter as dominant at the close of the seventeenth century one only was destined to survive the changes of the century and a half, and even the iconoclastic years, 1832–6, which, throughout nearly the whole range of Local Government, set the seal on the new principles by which the old ones were replaced. The fortunate survivor was the principle—in some respects actually strengthened by the Reformed Parliament—of the ownership of property, or at any rate the evidence of more than average fortune, as a necessary qualification for the exercise of governmental authority.

The dominance of this Property Qualification is seen most strikingly in the continued rule, in the Counties, of the Justices of the Peace. Apart from Middlesex and Surrey, in which the unregulated spread of the Metropolis had led, as we have described, to the degradation of the County Bench, the Commission of the Peace had everywhere remained restricted, with few exceptions, to the landowning class, to the exclusion of even wealthy ironmasters or merchants;

the squires being reinforced only by the leading rectors or vicars of the County, as owners of freehold benefices. In the early decades of the nineteenth century, in the struggle of the landed gentry to maintain a position of dominance in the nation, their class-exclusiveness became even more rigid.[1] Moreover, the clerical Justices of the type of the Rev. Henry Zouch, zealous for the 'reformation of manners' of the 'lower orders', incurred widespread unpopularity, not only among those with whose pleasures they interfered, but also among the 'friends of freedom' in all classes.[2] Even in the honest administration of their office, the Justices of the Peace made themselves, throughout the whole country, thoroughly disliked. Their attempts to regulate and limit the number of the inns and ale-houses were objected to, both as interfering with legitimate amusement and as violating the natural right of every man to invest his capital in any profit-making enterprise that he thought advantageous to himself. In their control of the local administration of the Poor

[1] Thus, in 1827, there was a great lack of magistrates in the mining districts of Monmouthshire; but the Lord-Lieutenant refused to recommend, for appointment to the County Bench, the younger son of an ironmaster who had become a landed proprietor. The heir apparent, it was explained, might be recommended, but not a younger son, even if he possessed the legal qualification (Duke of Beaufort to the Lord Chancellor, 16 November 1827; in MS. Home Office archives in Public Record Office).

[2] 'Most of the magistrates distinguished for over-activity are . . . clergymen' (Hansard, 1828, vol. xviii, N.S. p. 161). Windham was reported to have said 'that he did not know a more noxious species of vermin than an active Justice of the Peace' (*A Letter to the Rt. Hon. Lord Brougham and Vaux on the Magistracy of England*, 1832, p. 24; *The Parish and the County*, pp. 358–9).

Law, the Justices were objected to when they sought to limit the reckless generosity of the Vestry or the Overseer; and equally when, in the Allowance System, they strove to get the relief made adequate to the needs of each family. When they sought to obey the injunctions of Parliament, and to provide the County with decent prisons and lunatic asylums, not to say also to build the enlarged bridges that the growing traffic on the highroad required, they were denounced by all the ratepayers, and by most of the Radical reformers, for the rise of the rates that their 'extravagance' necessitated. But what more than anything else made the authority of the Justices unpopular among the masses of the people was the arbitrariness and severity with which they habitually administered the Game Laws, especially against any labourer suspected of poaching; and the reckless selfishness with which, particularly in the North of England after 1815, they abused their legal powers of stopping up the public footpaths that had from time immemorial crossed their estates. Meanwhile the wild panic which spread through the country houses of England, from the outbreak of the French Revolution onward—a panic maintained between 1816 and 1830 by the industrial and political unrest of the suffering wage-earning population—led to an administration of the Vagrancy Laws that can only be described as scandalously tyrannous. Any Justice of the Peace committed to prison any man or woman of the wage-earning class whom he chose to suspect of being of a seditious or even of a disturbing character. To the perpetual denunciations of the County Justices by the Philosophic Radicals and the rural ratepayers, there was thus added a furious underground hatred of these oppressors by the mass of factory operatives and farm labourers.[1]

Notwithstanding this widespread unpopularity of the Justices; notwithstanding the violation of all the cherished principles of Radicalism in the government and taxation of the County by the unrepresentative Court of Quarter Sessions; notwithstanding the very real shortcomings and limitations of these Rulers of the County, nothing was done to amend the constitution of the County Bench, and there was practically no proposal even for a removal of the Property Qualification.[2] What happened was the beginning of a process of erosion of the Justices' powers and functions, particularly as exercised by any single Justice, or pair of Justices. They were practically ousted in the decade following the Act of 1834 from the Poor Law administration; by the General Highways Act of 1835 they

[1] We believe that the state of feeling of the nation is accurately represented by the works of Mr. and Mrs. Hammond (*The Village Labourer*, *The Town Labourer* and *The Skilled Labourer*).

[2] By the Acts 13 Richard II, c. 7 and 2 Henry V, stat. 2, c. 1, Justices had to be made, within the County, of the most sufficient knights, esquires and gentlemen of the land. The qualification (for other than judges, peers and their heirs-apparent, or the heirs-apparent of landowners of at least £600 a year) was, by 5 George II, c. 18 and 18 George II, c. 20, fixed at the ownership of real estate producing at least £100 a year. Not until 1875 was the alternative qualification introduced of occupation within the County, for the preceding two years, of a dwelling-house rated at not less than £100 a year. This was removed by statute in 1901, when the qualification for a County Justice was made the same as that for a Borough Justice, namely the mere occupation of any rated premises, coupled with residence in or within seven miles; whilst all qualification except that of residence was removed in 1906.

lost the right of formally appointing the Surveyor of Highways and their practical power of directing the highway administration; they found themselves virtually excluded from the growing territory placed under the reformed Municipal Corporations, whilst, so far as civil administration was concerned, the Parishes in which Vestries were established under Hobhouse's Act were entirely abstracted from their control. The Prisons Act of 1835 made the magistrates definitely subordinate to the Home Office and its outspoken peripatetic inspectors. The Acts of 1836 and 1837 instituting a centralized system of registration of births, deaths and marriages, entirely ignored the Justices. With regard to their judicial functions, even within the territory left to them, their powers were successively restricted by the increasing transfer of their authority from the 'justice rooms' of their own mansions to the formal sittings of Petty Sessions 'in open Court', and by the greater opportunities of appeal to Quarter Sessions.[1] Nevertheless, in spite of this steady erosion of the structure of the Justices' power, it was still possible in the middle of the nineteenth century, for Rudolf von Gneist, in the successive editions of his account of English Local Government,[2] to regard the whole class

[1] This is not the place in which to describe the successive limitations of the Justices' functions during the remainder of the nineteenth century, culminating in 1888 in their practical supersession as administrators by the elective County Councils. What is here significant is that it was not until the twentieth century that the restrictive qualification for appointment to the Commission of the Peace was quite removed.

[2] *Adel und Ritterschaft in England*, 1853; *Geschichte und heutige Gestalt der Aemter in England*, 1857; *Die englische Communal-verfassung, oder das System des Self-Government*, 1860, 1863, 1871.

of country gentlemen, protected in their exclusive occupancy of the County Benches by the high property qualification, as the effective rulers of rural England.

In the other Local Authorities the prescribed qualification for office underwent, in the course of the eighteenth century, a gradual change, which became generalized during the first third of the nineteenth century. This change, whilst it significantly transformed the character of what we have called the Property Qualification, left it nevertheless effective as an instrument for the retention of authority by the relatively small minority of the population who constituted the propertied class. The first step was to admit, as an alternative qualification for certain offices, the ownership of a substantial amount not of property in land only, but of wealth of any kind. Alongside of this qualification by ownership of personal property was presently admitted, for some, and eventually for most offices, a qualification by mere occupancy, for a specified term, of a dwelling-house or other premises of a rateable value fixed at a figure so high as to exclude the vast majority of the inhabitants.

This introduction of a high rating qualification, or, indeed, any qualification at all beyond local inhabitancy, into the Local Government of the Parish was an innovation on behalf of the propertied class. No law had ever excluded any adult inhabitant from the Vestry meeting; and if, in all Parishes, the women abstained from attendance, and, in the rural Parishes, few if any labourers presumed to put in an appearance, this was merely a matter of use and wont. The open Vestry Meetings of Manchester and Leeds, Liverpool and Woolwich, which themselves decided the important issues of Parish administration, were attended by all classes of the inhabitants, rich or poor, and were even frequently dominated by 'the rabble'. Moreover, until the passing of Sturges Bourne's Act in 1819, each person in attendance, or voting in the poll taken as an adjournment of the Vestry meeting, had one vote, and one vote only. Similarly no law had prescribed any qualification (apart from special exemptions which were privileges), beyond that of residency, for the ancient office of Churchwarden, for which persons of the smallest fortune and of the humblest station, even Roman Catholics or Dissenters, were both eligible and liable to compulsory service. The case was the same for the statutory office of Overseer of the Poor, for which mere cottagers and day-labourers were held to be eligible and liable to service, even if only resident part of the year, and women equally with men, at least if no more 'substantial householders' were available.[1] There was just a beginning of a qualification for Parish office in 1691, when the Parish Officers and the inhabitants in Vestry assembled were required to present to the Justices a list of parishioners owning property, or at least occupiers of land or premises worth £30 a year, 'if such there be', and if not, 'of the most sufficient inhabitants', out of which the Justices were to appoint one or more Surveyors of Highways.[2]

[1] R. v. Stubbs, 2 T.R. 395, 406, etc.

[2] 3 William III, c. 12; re-enacted in 13 George III, c. 78, where it is further expressly specified that the Justices may, if the list contains none whom they think 'qualified', appoint any 'substantial inhabitants' living within the County and within three miles of the Parish.

Even in the Municipal Corporations, where power had, for the most part, fallen into the hands of small and usually close bodies, there continued, in some Boroughs, a relatively considerable class of Freemen, often consisting, to the extent of a majority, of manual-working wage-earners or otherwise indigent folk, who enjoyed, irrespective of whether or not they were occupying ratepayers, or whether they were rich or poor, the franchise for such elections as were held. In these Corporations, which included such extensive towns as Liverpool, Bristol, Norwich and Coventry, once a man had been admitted as a Freeman, whether by patrimony, apprenticeship, purchase or gift, he needed no other qualification, whatever his occupation, station or fortune, for appointment to any corporate office or dignity, not excluding that of membership of the close governing body, or the mayoralty itself. On the other hand, a non-Freeman remained in these Boroughs, right down to 1835, not only absolutely ineligible for any corporate office, however wealthy he might be, however extensive his business in the Borough, or however high the rateable value of the premises that he occupied; but also excluded from the valuable exemptions from tolls and dues, and the profitable right of sharing in the 'commons and stints' or other common property, enjoyed by his business rivals who were 'free' of the Corporation.

With regard to membership of a public body, it was naturally in the new Statutory Authorities for Special Purposes that the novel form of qualification came in. The Court of Sewers continued in this as in other respects closely to resemble the Court of Quarter Sessions.[1] For the membership of the Turnpike Trusts, however, we invariably find a statutory qualification, in which the ownership of £1,000 of personal property, or some other amount, was admitted as an alternative to the possession of an estate in land. In the Incorporated Guardians of the Poor, as we have seen, the qualification varied; but usually the County Justices and the Incumbents of benefices were reinforced not only by the owners of freehold estates, but also by the leaseholders (in which we think were included the farmers under any agreement of tenancy) of land worth at least £60 per annum. It is, however, in the more multifarious and diverse bodies of Commissioners for Paving, Lighting, Watching, Cleansing and otherwise Improving the various urban centres that we find both the greatest variety of qualification for office and the most obvious transition from the old forms of qualification to the new. Among the thousand Local Acts, by which, during the eighteenth century, the three hundred or so bodies of Commissioners were established or amended, there was introduced first the qualification of ownership of real estate; then the alternative of possession of £1,000 or other specified amount of any form of wealth; and in the later constitutions, first as a new alternative and latterly, in a few cases, as the only permissible form of qualification, the occupation within the town of premises of what

[1] The qualification for a Commissioner of Sewers, originally stated as land worth '40 marks' annually, and by 13 Elizabeth, c. 9 (1571) as forty pounds sterling, was actually raised in 1833 to £100 a year freehold, or £200 a year leasehold, within the County (3 & 4 William IV, c. 22).

was at the time a high annual value[1]—sometimes (as in Manchester in 1828) £28 per annum, sometimes twice that sum, which, in the early part of the century, indicated the shop or warehouse of a very substantial trader or the mansion of a man of wealth.

With regard to the qualification for the franchise, it was a characteristic feature of the Local Government reforms of the first third of the nineteenth century, that, along with the privileges of the Freemen in the Municipal Corporations, the remaining laxity as to qualification in Parish administration was brought to an end.[2] It became the general rule that no one should exercise any right to vote, and in most cases, that no one should be eligible for any elective office, unless his name was actually entered in the ratebook as that of a ratepayer, whether as occupier or as owner, of premises within the area concerned. Alike for the Parish Committees under Sturges Bourne's Act, for the elective Vestries under Hobhouse's Act, for the Boards of Guardians under the regulations made upon the authority of the Poor Law Amendment Act, for the Town Councils under the Municipal Corporations Act, and even for the Highway Committees under the General Highways Act, it was taken for granted, when

[1] It is curious to find the requirement that publicans, to be eligible, needed a rating qualification twice as great as other inhabitants.

[2] The strenuous fight of the House of Lords against the Municipal Corporations Bill in its original form maintained the vote, for the new Town Councils, of the possibly non-occupying, indigent and even pauper Freemen of Liverpool, Coventry and other ancient Boroughs, so far as the existing holders of privileges were concerned, though the Act abolished the privilege as regards future generations.

not expressly laid down by regulation or statute, that the franchise was confined to independent occupiers of dwelling-houses or other premises, whose names were on the ratebook as direct payers of the local rates, and whose rates during the prescribed period had been actually paid. The prescribed period of occupancy and ratepaying was, in some cases (as by the Municipal Corporations Act (fixed at two years next previous to the making of the last rate. And when to this was added the disfranchisement, not merely of those householders who were aliens, but also (for Boards of Guardians) of all persons who (or any member of whose family) had received during the prescribed period any kind of parochial relief, and (for the new Town Councils) of all occupiers of the female sex—when it is realized that it became an almost universal practice of the landlord of small cottage property or tenement dwellings himself to pay the rates, and thus keep all his tenants off the ratebook—it will be seen how very far was the franchise for the elective Local Authorities, even after the reforms of 1832–6, from that of a universal Democracy of Consumers. Exact statistics do not exist, but it is probable that the aggregate electorate of all the elective Local Authorities of England and Wales did not, in 1836, for a population then amounting to over 14 millions, or some three million families, exceed the total number of Parliamentary electors, which is commonly estimated at 800,000. Speaking generally, it may be said that, whereas at the end of the seventeenth century, every householder, male or female, could legally attend and vote at the Parish Vestry, and in the Municipal

Corporations even the poorest Freeman was a member of the Corporation; after the Local Government revolution of 1818–36 only one householder out of four could cast a vote.[1]

But the restriction of the Local Government franchise to those who had been, over a prescribed period, directly assessed to, and had actually paid the local rates, with the further disfranchisement of aliens, paupers, married women and (for the Town Councils) even independent women ratepayers, was not the whole of the establishment of what amounted virtually to a new Property Qualification. By Sturges Bourne's Act of 1819, followed by the much more important Poor Law Amendment Act of 1834, as amended by that of 1844, the device of Plural Voting was introduced in such a way as to place the dominant power even more certainly in the hands of the richer inhabitants. Each registered owner (who might be only a leaseholder of a mortgagee), and each rated occupier of the premises in the ratebook, was accorded, in the election of the Poor Law Authority, from one up to six votes, according to the annual value of the premises, with the further aggravation that where (as became usual with all cottage property or tenement dwellings) the landlord's name appeared on the ratebook as owner and also as paying the rates for his tenants, he enjoyed double votes, thus being given as much as twelve times the weight of such occupants of the smaller dwellings as had votes at all. At the same time statutory provision

[1] It is something more than a coincidence that the proportion of weekly wage-earners and their families to the whole population certainly amounted to three-fourths.

was made in 1844 to enable joint stock companies or other corporate bodies to vote as persons, and individual owners were even enabled to send an agent to cast their votes for their property, with the singular proviso that 'except a tenant, bailiff, steward, land-agent or collector of rents', no such agent was allowed to cast votes on behalf of more than four owners![1] Here, perhaps, is found the most ingenious application of the principle of Property Qualification for the exercise of authority, seeing that it secured the predominance of the propertied class in the State without necessarily involving the exclusion of even the poorest resident. The most straightforward defence of this device of plural voting, because it shows how the commercialized political philosophy of the time had spread even to the oldest English aristocracy, is that made by Lord Salisbury in resisting the coming of Household Suffrage. His daughter, Lady Gwendolen Cecil, describing and quoting from his article on the subject in 1864, thus summarizes his argument: 'A democratic extension of the franchise would not only give a share to every man in the government of the country, but would give to every man an equal share. *Yet with regard to the chief subject-matter of Parliamentary action* [the italics are ours], there is, and always will be, a ubiquitous inequality of interest in the decisions taken. He suggests an analogy in the management of joint-stock companies. The best test of natural right is that right which mankind, left to themselves to regulate their own concerns, most naturally admit. Joint-stock companies, like States, finding themselves too numerous to undertake

[1] 7 & 8 Vict., c. 101, sec. 15 (1844).

directly the management of their affairs, have adopted a representative system. How do they settle this thorny question of the suffrage? The system under which, by universal agreement, such bodies are universally managed is that the voting power should be strictly proportioned to the stake which each man holds in the company. It is a system whose justice has never been disputed. The question has never even been a matter of controversy. The wildest dreamer never suggested that all the shareholders should each have a single vote without reference to the number of shares they might hold.'[1]

If it is significant to find the Cecil of 1864 unhesitatingly assuming that the 'chief subject-matter of Parliamentary action' is the maintenance of private property (for it is in this only that there can be said to be 'a ubiquitous inequality of interest in the decisions taken'), it is interesting to see how mistaken he proved to be in supposing that 'mankind left to themselves' invariably adopted the joint-stock principle of voting according to the amount of wealth at stake. The consumers' Co-operative Movement, which was, in 1864, in its infancy, now (1922) includes in its membership in the United Kingdom some four million households, or more than a third of the total. These men and women, far more numerous than the entire aggregate of shareholders in joint-stock companies, and owning

[1] *Life of the Marquis of Salisbury*, by Lady Gwendolen Cecil, 1921, vol. 8, p. 152. It may be recalled that Burke had declared that 'Property . . . never can be safe from the invasion of ability unless it be, out of all proportion, dominant in the representation' (*Reflections on the French Revolution*).

among them over £100,000,000 worth of capital in their Co-operative Movement—have always, spontaneously and unquestioningly, adopted in the constitution of the Co-operative world, the principle of 'One Member one Vote', irrespective, not only of age and sex, station or fortune, but also of the amount of share or loan capital possessed by each.[1]

The qualification for public office was, in certain cases, even more restrictive in its effects than that for the franchise. Thus the Poor Law Commissioners, in framing their regulations for the new Boards of Guardians under the Poor Law Amendment Act, which had empowered the fixing of a rating qualification not exceeding £40 a year, willingly adopted this statutory maximum for all the Unions in the the Metropolitan area, and for some of those elsewhere, whilst in all Unions whatever such a rating qualification was fixed as to exclude not only the whole wage-earning class, and all the smaller shopkeepers, but also, incidentally, most of the independent women occupiers.[2]

We may point out that there was the less need, in the nineteenth as in the twentieth century, for any such rigid exclusion from office of the four-fifths or seven-eighths of the adult population who could not prove either their ownership of landed or other property, or

[1] *The Consumers' Co-operative Movement*, by S. and B Webb, 1921.

[2] The rating qualification for Guardians was not reduced until 1893, when it was fixed at £5 only. It needed another statute to abolish the qualification altogether; see Local Government Act, 1894, sec. 20 (5). Even then, the qualification of £40 remained (and still remains) for membership of the Metropolitan Aylums Board for anyone not possessing real estate within the area.

even their occupancy of a dwelling-house rated at £40 a year, in that service in the elected offices was almost invariably unpaid. The whole aggregate of persons in industrial or commercial employment at wages or salaries, together with all those in the service of public bodies, and all the more necessitous shopkeepers and other employers or professional men, were (as they still are) normally excluded from the elective Local Authorities by their inability to give the necessary time. The refusal to provide either salary or fees for the members of local governing bodies, even such merely as would pay for the time actually spent on the public service, amounts in itself practically to the maintenance of a Property Qualification, which, without any further restriction, necessarily confines membership to the small minority who are able and willing to afford such a sacrifice of their time. The actual result has been, in the nineteenth century, to throw the Town Councils and Boards of Guardians almost entirely into the hands, not of the largest and wealthiest merchants and traders, any more than of the landowners or of the mass of wage-earners, but of the substantial resident shopkeepers, builders and publicans in the towns, and farmers in the country, with a small intermixture of auctioneers, petty contractors, and here and there a few solicitors, doctors or persons retired from business. Apart from the Courts of Quarter Sessions and the Courts of Sewers, English Local Government was, by the series of reforms that culminated in 1836, in effect handed over, almost exclusively, to a particular stratum of the middle class.

But Still no System of Local Government

We end our analysis of the new principles that emerged in English Local Government between the Revolution and the Municipal Corporations Act, on the same note as we struck in opening our previous chapter. In 1836, as in 1689, there was still nothing in Local Government that could be called a system. The separate forms of social organization, the Manor and the Borough, the Parish and the County, originating indifferently in prescription and local custom, charter and Royal Commission, Common Law and Parliamentary statute, superimposed one on top of another according to the needs and circumstances of each century, and inextricably entangled in each other's growth and decay, had been made even more complicated and confused by the establishment, during the eighteenth and early nineteenth centuries, of the eighteen hundred new Statutory Authorities for Special Purposes, only partially connected with the constitution and activities of the other local institutions that we have described. By Sturges Bourne's Act and Hobhouse's Act, the Poor Law Amendment Act and the Municipal Corporations Act, the General Highways Act and the Births and Deaths Registration Acts, this heterogeneous complex of overlapping Local Authorities was not straightened out into any systematic organization. Not one of the fifteen thousand or more separate local governing bodies found itself actually abolished, even by the most iconoclastic of these statutes. What these Acts accomplished was finally to dispossess the old principles

—save for certain surviving remnants—and to set the seal upon the adoption, in the reorganized bodies to which all authority was gradually transferred, of the new principles that we have described. But no organic system of Local Government as a whole could at that time be recognized. The Metropolitan Vestries, the Parish Committees of provincial Vestries, the Municipal Corporations, the new Boards of Guardians, not to mention such survivals as the Courts of Sewers, the Turnpike Trusts and the Improvement Commissioners, the still existing City of London and other unreformed Corporations, and such ephemeral Authorities as the Local Boards of Health and the Highway Boards, had, without reference to each other, all been created or reformed by separate statutes, to meet particular circumstances. Their methods of election were unlike. The qualifications for the franchise and for office differed materially and irrationally from one to the other. The areas over which the several Authorities exercised their diverse jurisdictions overlapped each other; their several powers and functions were sometimes inconsistent and frequently duplicated; they levied on the same ratepayers a multitude of different imposts, assessed under different rules, and payable at different dates. The position of these multifarious Local Authorities to each other was undefined; whilst their relations to the National Executive were as diverse as their constitutions or their functions. Thus, whilst the Municipal Corporations, like the rural Parish Vestries, had the very minimum of contact with any Government Department, and were subject to practically no control, the new Boards of Guardians were bound hand and foot to the autocratic Poor Law Commissioners; in their administration of the Births, Marriages and Deaths Registration Acts the new Local Authorities had to obey the commands of the Registrar-General; and even the Courts of Quarter Sessions were, in respect of their prison administration, brought under the peremptory injunctions of the Home Office.

What was effected in 1832–6, so far as English Local Government was concerned, was definitely to cut it off from Vocational Organization, with its exclusiveness, industrial, political or religious; its methods of Co-option and of universal rotational tenure of public office, and above all its assumption that the direction of any service should be vested in those who performed it—and to base the new bodies on election by a ratepayers' or consumers' Democracy, in which those who enjoyed the benefit of the public services, and paid for them by local taxation, were themselves assumed to exercise all authority through their elected representatives, who ordered and directed the work of contractors or paid servants. It was, as we can now see, this form of government that was destined, in the course of the nineteenth century, to become universal. It is on the basis of this Ratepayers' Democracy of 1832–6, completed as a Consumers' Democracy by the franchise or rating reforms of 1867, 1869, 1888, 1894, 1900, 1917, and 1918, that English Local Government, after a further three-quarters of a century of effort, has ceased to be the chaos of areas, chaos of Authorities and chaos of rates, which it was left in 1836; and has at last, in the twentieth century, become, as Francis Place predicted, fairly well systematized in the municipal form.

Unfortunately, as we have seen, the reforms of 1832–6 failed not only to systematize Local Government, but also—mainly by the froward retention of the old principle of Property Qualification in its new guise—failed to make the Ratepayers' Democracy coextensive with the consumers of the public services which it had collectively to provide. By the ratepaying qualification, nearly always fixed at a high figure, coupled with the refusal of any payment for public work, the framers of the legislation of 1818–36 not only excluded from the reformed Councils, as they intended, the manual-working class, and, indeed, the great mass of folk of all occupations absorbed in earning a livelihood, but also, as was probably not foreseen, practically the men of wider education, the brain-working professions, the heads of the more important businesses, and all others who did not actually reside within the particular ward or local district for which representatives had to be elected. Incidentally all women, whether married or unmarried, were long debarred, either by law or by the practice of the rating Authorities, from serving on any public bodies. The result was that nearly the whole of Local Government, outside the restricted scope of the Courts of Quarter Sessions and the Courts of Sewers, was handed over to the class of retail shopkeepers and farmers, whose virtues, whose shortcomings and whose general outlook on life became everywhere dominant, alike in the Town Council, in the Parish Vestry and in the Board of Guardians. We cannot express it better than in the carefully weighed judgment—already quoted by us in connexion with the relatively democratic Corporation of the City of London, and full of significance to students of political science—which De Tocqueville passed upon the government of France between 1830 and 1848. The dominating spirit of that government, he said, was the spirit characteristic of the trading Middle Class; a spirit active and assiduous; always narrow; often corrupt; occasionally, through vanity or egotism, insolent, but by temperament timid; mediocre and moderate in all things except in the enjoyment of physical indulgence; a spirit which, when combined with the spirit of the manual-working wage-earners and the spirit of the aristocracy, may achieve marvels, but which, taken alone, inevitably produces a government without elevation and without quality.[1] We may add a significant comment on the Local Government of the generation that followed immediately on the reforms of 1832–6 by a well-instructed official. 'Too often', said Tom Taylor, who had been Secretary to the Central Board of Health, ' "local self-government" is another name for the unchecked rule of the least informed, noisiest and narrowest, or, as often, of the most self-seeking, who can achieve seats in a Town Council or at a Local Improvement Board. . . . But, in the whirl of complicated affairs, among the incessant demands of private interests stimulated by the closest competition, the bewildering action and counter action of class wants and claims, and the self-consciousness bred of too exclusive a pursuit of material advancement,

[1] *Souvenirs d'Alexis de Tocqueville*, 1893, p. 6 (freely translated); *The Manor and the Borough*, p. 692.

it is no wonder if the most public-spirited, the most anxious to do their best for the interests of the community of which they are a part, who often find themselves more and more perplexed and baffled, and discover, to their dismay, that active participation in local affairs too often resolves itself into an unsuccessful struggle with the grossest ignorance, the most offensive mob oratory, and the most sordid self-seeking. Only very stout hearts indeed can long maintain the struggle. The temptation is too often irresistible to withdraw from the Town Council or Local Board, and to seek in the exercise of more secluded benevolence for a satisfaction of those inward urgings to unselfish duty which can find no useful employment in the public arena without.'[1]

Such is the pessimistic verdict of a competent observer of 1857. But no judicial estimate of the nature and results of the revolutionary transformation of the machinery of Local Government effected in 1832–6 could be made in that generation. It would be misleading and unfair to leave off on Tom Taylor's depressing note. A popular dramatist turned bureaucrat, grappling with the 'Early Victorian' stupidities of local officials, and the prejudices of the average sensual man, could hardly be expected to take an optimistic view of Local Government. It is more instructive to consider the exceptional difficulties with which the new elective bodies had to cope. For it must be remembered

1 'On Central and Local Action in Relation to Town Improvement', by Tom Taylor, M.A., in *Transactions of the National Association for the Promotion of Social Science*, 1857, p. 475. Tom Taylor proceeds to suggest the importance of central control.

that all the disastrous changes in the environment of the common people, due to the Industrial Revolution described in the opening pages of this chapter, continued in operation, in some cases with accelerating speed, during the whole of the first half of the nineteenth century, and even later. The population, in spite of (and perhaps because of) widespread destitution and servitude, went on increasing, and more and more crowding into the urban slums. The devastating torrent of nuisances, characteristic of unrestricted profit-making enterprise, went on spreading over the land, maintaining the sickness-rate, the accident-rate and the death-rate at appallingly high figures, whilst the insanitary factories and workshops, and the unregulated mines and smelting works were insidiously lowering the vitality of men, women and children. To guide the new Local Authorities there was no administrative science. There was no fully organized National Executive charged with protecting the race from the worst results of the capitalist system. Not until the last quarter of the nineteenth century, and then only imperfectly, can even the educated public be said to have realized the necessity for the legal limitation and regulation of capitalist enterprise; nor can our Factory and Workshop Acts, Mines Regulation Acts and Merchant Shipping Acts be said to have more than begun to ensure to the whole population that fundamental National Minimum of the conditions of civilized life without which Local Government can be no more than a botch. And the instruments were as lacking as the science and the law. To replace the ordinary citizen temporarily conscripted to unpaid public service, there was, in 1835, no body of trustworthy, trained, professional officials. The specially characteristic modern vocations, whether of engineers, architects, surveyors, accountants, and auditors; or of teachers, nurses, sanitary inspectors and medical officers of health; or even of draughtsmen, bookkeepers, clerks and policemen, were as yet only beginning to be developed. Without effective vocational organization they were still without either tradition or training, and wholly unprovided with the code of professional ethics on which, as we now know, the highest administrative efficiency so much depends. The obsolescent and obstructive medieval vocational organization had been cleared out of the way; and the new and virile type of vocational organization, of which the germs lay in the then persecuted and prescribed Trade Union Movement and the beginnings of modern Professional Association, had not yet been created.

No less important was the nature of the functions to which the nascent Local Government of the nineteenth century was still confined. By far the most extensive service was, for several decades after 1836, that of the relief of the poor. Now, necessary as may have been the Poor Law revolution of 1834, and devoted as were the services of many of those who worked at its administration, it proved impossible to enlist either administrative genius or public support for a purely deterrent and repressive treatment of destitution and vagrancy. Scarcely more inspiring seemed municipal government, so long as this was confined, in the main, to the suppression of those nuisances which threatened the health or lessened the amenity of the life of the Middle

Class. It took, we may usefully remember, all the rest of the nineteenth century to generalize and extend to the whole field of Local Government, even the structural reforms of 1832–6. It was at least as long before the new Local Government got into its stride as the obligatory Association of Consumers for the collective provision of those services and commodities for which profit-making enterprise seemed less well adapted than communal organization. With the gradual assumption, as communal services, of the whole range of education from the nursery school to the university; of the organization in parks and open spaces, in libraries and museums, in music rooms and picture galleries, of recreation and amusement; of a general provision, not merely for the treatment of the sick, but also actually for the promotion of health of future generations as well as of the present; of town planning, local transport and housing not merely as the correctives of slums but as the creators of the city of tomorrow; and, last but by no means least, of the supply of water, gas, electricity, power, and local transportation as necessary adjuncts of municipal life, the whole scope and spirit of Local Government has been transformed. Merely in magnitude and range of affairs the Local Government of 1922 is much further removed from that of 1836, than that of 1836 was from its predecessor of 1689. The ten or twelve millions sterling of annual revenue of all the English Local Authorities on the accession of Queen Victoria have become the three hundred million pounds of gross receipts of the Local Authorities of today; the few thousand persons whom they employed, for the most part contractors and low-paid labour, have grown into an average staff, at salaries or wages, of something like a million on the pay roll of 1922, comprising as many as one in fifteen of the entire working population; whilst the capital administered by the various Local Authorities of England and Wales, formerly infinitesimal, now exceeds in value 1,500 millions sterling. With this growth of Local Government in magnitude and variety; and especially with its expansion from essentially repressive or eleemosynary functions into the communal organization of the city life, new classes have reinforced the municipal service, both as elected representatives and as officials. The wage-earning class has, in the twentieth century, not only supplied from its educated children the great bulk of the new hierarchy of Local Government staffs; but has also, by electing to the Councils its Trade Union officials, and sometimes by providing for its representatives a modest salary, increasingly managed to overcome the barrier presented by Property Qualification and the Non-Payment of Councillors. And Local Government in its modern guise, with its new and larger aims and vaster problems, has come to attract, both as elected representatives and as officials, ever more and more of the ablest and best trained intellects, who find, in its service, whether paid or unpaid, an inspiration and a scope actually superior, in their own estimation, to that offered by the pursuit of pecuniary profit. In short, English Local Government, in 1832–6 handed over, in effect, to a particular stratum of the Middle Class, has gradually become representative of all the best sections of English life.

But this story is not for us to tell. How from the

unsystematized and, as we have indicated, 'commercialized' chaos of separate Authorities of 1836, English Local Government has, in the course of three-quarters of a century, become generally organized as a Consumers' Democracy; how the invidious and, as we think, calamitous exclusion of the great mass of the consumers has been, by a whole series of minor reforms of franchise and rating, largely remedied; how the merely eleemosynary and largely deterrent 'relief of destitution' has been, in one department after another, replaced by the institution of communal services, and the demoralizing Poor Law Authority increasingly superseded by municipal activities; how new vocational organization has arisen to redeem an untempered consumers' government, and the necessary provision—absolutely ignored in 1836—for the participation in the administration of those who are actually engaged in the service is, in the twentieth century, at least beginning to be made; how the still unsolved problems of areas, of the equalization of burdens, and of the relation between local and central Authorities are being tentatively explored; how with this greater inclusiveness and with the elaboration of an administrative science the outlook and purpose of Local Government has been gradually defined, widened and ennobled—all this fascinating evolution of Parish and Borough and County into the Local Government of today we must regretfully leave to be described by younger students.

INDEX

Printed in Great Britain by
The Camelot Press Ltd., London and Southampton